THE RED CADDY

ALSO BY CHARLES BOWDEN

Killing the Hidden Waters (1977)

Street Signs Chicago: Neighborhood and Other Illusions of Big-City Life,
  with Lewis Kreinberg and Richard Younker (1981)

Blue Desert (1986)

Frog Mountain Blues, with Jack W. Dykinga (1987)

Trust Me: Charles Keating and the Missing Billions,
  with Michael Binstein (1988)

Mezcal (1988)

Red Line (1989)

Desierto: Memories of the Future (1991)

The Sonoran Desert, with Jack W. Dykinga (1992)

The Secret Forest, with Jack W. Dykinga and Paul S. Martin (1993)

Seasons of the Coyote: The Legend and Lore of an American Icon,
  with Philip L. Harrison (1994)

Blood Orchid: An Unnatural History of America (1995)

Chihuahua: Pictures From the Edge, with Virgil Hancock (1996)

Stone Canyons of the Colorado Plateau, with Jack W. Dykinga (1996)

Juárez: The Laboratory of our Future,
  with Noam Chomsky and Eduardo Galeano (1998)

Eugene Richards, with Eugene Richards (2001)

Down by the River: Drugs, Money, Murder, and Family (2002)

Blues for Cannibals: The Notes from Underground (2002)

A Shadow in the City: Confessions of an Undercover Drug Warrior (2005)

Inferno, with Michael P. Berman (2006)

Exodus/Éxodo, with Julián Cardona (2008)

Some of the Dead are Still Breathing: Living in the Future (2009)

Trinity, with Michael P. Berman (2009)

*Murder City: Ciudad Juárez and the Global Economy's
  New Killing Fields* (2010)

Dreamland: The Way Out of Juárez, with Alice Leora Briggs (2010)

The Charles Bowden Reader (2010)

El Sicario: The Autobiography of a Mexican Assassin,
  Molly Molloy, co-editor (2011)

CHARLES BOWDEN
THE RED CADDY

Into the Unknown with
EDWARD ABBEY

Foreword by
LUIS ALBERTO URREA

University of Texas Press ⌄ Austin

Lannan
CHARLES BOWDEN PUBLISHING PROJECT

Copyright © 2018 by the Charles Clyde Bowden Literary Trust
Mary Martha Miles, Trustee
Foreword copyright © 2018 by Luis Alberto Urrea
All rights reserved
Printed in the United States of America
First edition, 2018

Requests for permission to reproduce material from this work should be sent to:
    Permissions
    University of Texas Press
    P.O. Box 7819
    Austin, TX 78713-7819
    utpress.utexas.edu/rp-form

♾ The paper used in this book meets the minimum requirements of ANSI/NISO
Z39.48-1992 (R1997) (Permanence of Paper).

Library of Congress Cataloging-in-Publication Data
Names: Bowden, Charles, 1945–2014, author. | Urrea, Luis Alberto, writer of
supplementary textual content.
Title: The red caddy : into the unknown with Edward Abbey / Charles Bowden ;
foreword by Luis Alberto Urrea.
Description: First edition. | Austin : University of Texas Press, 2018.
Identifiers: LCCN 2017039368
  ISBN 978-1-4773-1579-8 (cloth : alk. paper)
  ISBN 978-1-4773-1580-4 (library e-book)
  ISBN 978-1-4773-1581-1 (non-library e-book)
Subjects: LCSH: Abbey, Edward, 1927–1989. | Authors, American—20th century—
Biography. | Novelists, American—20th century—Biography. | Environmentalists—
United States—Biography.
Classification: LCC PS3551.B2 Z595 2018 | DDC 813/.54 [B] —dc23
LC record available at https://lccn.loc.gov/2017039368
doi:10.7560/315798

For the Lone Ranger who is still out there toiling away on the graveyard shift, and for all my fellow Tontos

The simple telescope, for instance, has given us visions of a world far greater, lovelier, more awesome and full of wonder than that contained in an entire shipload of magic mushrooms, LSD capsules, and yoga textbooks. But . . . that science in our time is the whore of industry and the slut of war, and that scientific technology has become the instrument of potential planetary slavery, the most powerful weapon ever placed in the hands of despots.

Edward Abbey, *The Best of Edward Abbey*

But there was nothing out there. Nothing at all. Nothing but desert. Nothing but the silent world. *That's why.*

And no man sees. No woman hears. No one is there. Everything is there.

Edward Abbey, *The Journey Home: Some Words in Defense of the American West*

. . . The desert is also a-tonal, cruel, clear, inhuman, neither romantic nor classical, motionless and emotionless, at one and the same time—another paradox—both agonized and deeply still. Like death? Perhaps.

Edward Abbey, *Desert Solitaire*

Right, he will yell, you got it. He'll pull her small body firmly to his side, steer back onto the pavement, press the pedal to the floor.

The big brute motor will grumble like a lion, old, tired, hesitating, then catch fire and roar, eight-hearted in its block of iron, driving onward, westward always, into the sun . . .

Edward Abbey, *The Fool's Progress: An Honest Novel*

The License Plate Said "Hayduke": Chuck Bowden and the Red Cadillac

A Memory by Luis Alberto Urrea

> I try to construct a theory of how a moral person should live in these
> circumstances, and how such a person should love.
>
> Charles Bowden, *Desierto*

I

"Love" might not be the first thing that comes to mind when one considers the often angry, hard-bitten books Charles Bowden wrote. But love was what burned inside him, it seemed to me.

Those who knew him far better than I have told me this more than once. Even the ones who are still mad at him. Even Jim Harrison, after Bowden had left this earth.

I don't think he was claiming to be a moral person, in this quote. But I do believe he was trying his damnedest to live by a code. It just had to be a code of his own devising. I risked calling him my friend.

This is how the thing began.

Early in February of 1993, between 6:00 and 7:00 in the morning, my phone rang. I was hiding out in San Diego after a doomed marriage had fallen apart behind me. And my first book had been on the shelves for less than a month. It was a nonfiction account of my previous life working with the disadvantaged people of my birthplace, Tijuana.

I scrambled for the receiver before the answering machine kicked in. The Voice, the voice his many friends and enemies and paramours would never forget, spoke.

"Urrea?" it said.

My first impression: the guy got the pronunciation right. My second impression: he was some crusty tough guy who sounded hungover. Some character out of a B. Traven novel.

"It's Bowden."

Wait. What? As in Charles Bowden?

"Yeah. It's Chuck."

I was immediately pacing the floor.

"Where are you?" he said.

I was trying to wake up enough to understand that Charles Bowden had tracked me down for some reason.

I started to tell him he was one of my prose heroes. Then I remembered to answer his question. "San Diego," I said.

"What the hell are you doing *there*?"

I went into the marriage falling apart explanation.

He cut me off.

"I know about those," he said. "Where were you living before San Diego?"

He said *San Diego* as if it hurt his soul.

"Boulder, Colorado."

There was a long pause. I imagined him taking a drink, or taking a drag on a cigarette.

"Jesus," he said, "talk about a place that makes you want to commit suicide."

Bowden followed this comment with marching orders.

"Where you need to live is in Tucson."

He said something about Boulder being an amusement park for rich people and that it had trucks gluing up picturesque claptrap all over town to make those people feel special.

Both Bowden's and Ed Abbey's books were on the shelf beside my phone. A devil's claw sat beside my computer. Tucson. It would have seemed insane to think I had just heard Chuck suggesting, "Come be my friend." An invitation to take the first step into Bowdenworld. But that's how I took it. His real friends could have told me he was also saying, "Come here and let me kick your ass."

I had been infatuated with Edward Abbey for years. I was one of those who had camped in deserts often as a kid, and now fancied myself some kind of Abbeyesque long-haul dry-lands wanderer. (I had a much milder demeanor than Ed—every time I reread *The Monkey Wrench Gang*, I grew afraid that the FBI was going to bust through my windows and arrest me for subversion. And then there was that Mexican-hating thing of Abbey's.) But reading his work opened the door to Bowden.

When I read *Blue Desert*, I thought it was one of the greatest American books of the modern era. I distributed Chuck's chapter on bats and their caves to writing students who often stared at it in bewilderment. Like, bats? I may or may not have known that Ed and Chuck were dear friends at that time. Though Chuck would have never stooped to an adjective like "dear." I learned that if he sounded like he could barely stand you, he loved you on some level.

Re: friendship with Abbey, Bowden writes: *He was reasonably polite, didn't shit on the floor, and was well read.*

Selah.

In that first phone call, Bowden announced: "You owe me money."

"I do?"

"Forty bucks."

I must have laughed. I had no idea what was happening.

He said, "I've been up all night rereading your book. And I've bought copies for all my friends."

I somehow knew it was true.

In *The Red Caddy*, Bowden implies that to be an expert on your friend means you were never really that person's friend at all. I didn't know this. I wandered around pondering the weird phone call from the icon. I went to the bookstore to hunt for any new or old Bowdens I hadn't read. They were almost impossible to find, and it made them more appealing. But I was trying to be an expert. That never impressed him.

I had a Jeep, no job, and a little bit of publisher money in my pocket. I packed up and headed for Tucson. Time to meet the master.

I decided to bring an outlaw with me.

This monster of a man had been a biker once, and he boasted of having sex with a woman while stoned and speeding up I-5 on a Harley. He had also guarded LSD loads with a shotgun for the Hells Angels. He sported a Grizzly Adams beard and a head scarf, and was now a born-again Christian who was featured in my border book. Talk about a Bowden character.

Knowing Bowden's penchant for outrage at the vagaries of this world, I also thought he'd be moved to learn that the biker was ultimately too wild for his church. That his beloved congregation had turned on him and turned him out. After years of service feeding the poor in Mexico, he was homeless and living out of public restrooms in San Diego. So I'd gone and collected him and moved him into my back bedroom.

Let's call him Bear.

I called Chuck and told him we were on our way. He did not seem surprised. Over the years, it seemed very important to Chuck that nothing could be seen to surprise him. He allowed books to do that, but few people got the chance.

He told me to meet him at a bar on the corner of Speedway and Campbell. It was in a big hotel because witnesses would make it harder for the narco hitmen to get him. I laughed. What a card. He didn't laugh. He told me there would be a bodyguard. I stopped laughing.

The bar no longer exists. This is fitting. The message of *The Red Caddy*, for all its gloriously hard-bitten prose and philosophical tough-guy narrative, and its often hilarious bluster, is a deep shade of melancholy. A sense of mortality that shadows the pages like the slow creep of dusk sliding over the desert. The bar is gone, its hotel is gone, Ed Abbey is gone, Bear is gone, Chuck is gone, and the bodyguard is gone.

Bear and I walked in and were greeted with a hard-boiled scene from some '50s detective movie. There sat Bowden, back to the wall. Looking wrinkled and beat and nursing a beer. His sideburns were white. I think he was smoking.

Standing to his left, leaning on the wall, was a deadly look-ing older Mexican with his arms crossed. The man gave us the stink-eye and looked past us. The whole time, he scanned the empty bar for evildoers. "Ex-Federal," Bowden said. "Armed." He shook our hands and called for three more beers. With limes.

He told us some convoluted tale of Mexican narcos who were mad at him over some slight, either in his writing or his general comportment. Perhaps a dustup at a narcotraficante ranch, and there might have been a party involved. I don't remember now, I was too amazed by this scenario, and keeping my eye on the gunman. Bowden advised me to always sit with my back to a wall so nobody could sneak up and assassinate me.

I half expected gunfire to erupt without warning. Which Chuck might have wanted me to think, just to see how I would act. Suddenly, all this manhood struck me as hilariously silly. Chuck gave all evidence of being in on the joke. The prospect of being shot by sicarios seemed to make him feel full of pep.

Tucson old-timers, by the way, will know that the bodyguard was the indestructible Art Carrillo Strong, author of *Corrido de Cocaine*.

"You two fed the poor, huh?" Chuck said, staring at Bear.

He was more interested in him than he was in me. Writers? He knew a million. And the writers he knew were not just typists but pistoleros. Biker missionary outlaw homeless guys, though, were something new.

Chuck leaned across the table and stared at Bear. He finally said, "Bear, are you a good man?"

"Good?"

Bear twitched and fidgeted and looked away.

"I don't know," he said.

It was a direct kung-fu strike.

Bear drained his beer and went looking for another.

Thinking I'd turn the conversational tables on Bowden, I said, "Was Ed Abbey a good man?"

Chuck looked at his hands splayed on the table.

Then he started to cry.

He muttered something like "Fuck this" and walked out of the bar.

How should such a person love?

II

I didn't see Bowden again for a year. Eventually, we were both booked to speak at a panel at a southwestern university. I was unsure of my standing with the great man. But he was the kind of guy, in my experience, who liked you to think he lived in the moment and didn't worry about old weepy episodes. When I walked toward the auditorium, he was sprawled on a bench outside, looking more disreputable than he had in the bar. His idea of dressing up. Three women hovered around him, getting autographs. He was in great spirits, flirting in an offhanded way that had them riveted. He greeted me enthusiastically and began an impromptu lecture about the Mexican Revolution that lasted for about twenty minutes. He handed me a copy of Daniel Nugent's *Spent Cartridges of Revolution*. "Read this if you want to understand about revolution," he said. I still have it.

Inside, we sat at a long, swooping table laden with microphones and pitchers of ice water. I remember it as some vast gathering, dozens of scholars, but I'm sure there were only five or six of us at the table and maybe a hundred people in the audience. We each gave our perspectives on the border. Scholars droned on and on, it's true. Footnotes were parsed. Bowden, who never met a gangster he didn't love, even when the killers he dropped in his pages gave every indication of having been kids lounging around a Juarez barrio out of boredom, painted his usual ghastly border inferno. How could you argue with him? He was a force of nature. He was being hunted by narcos, for God's sake.

Being born in Tijuana, and having lived all my life on both sides of the border fence—sometimes in both places at once—I had what I considered to be a saner view of that hideous death trap that so appalled observers of the border. After all, I argued, those of us who live with it every day also see it as a symbol of family, of potential, perhaps even as a place where two cultures might meet each other in partnership as well as conflict. Witness the Mexican and American kids who regularly play volleyball over parts of the wall. And it was evident that a new renaissance in commerce, technology, culture and the arts was coming.

I was saying this, apparently to Chuck's exasperation.

Suddenly, he took up his microphone to interrupt me.

"I don't know what planet you're from," he drawled.

Laughter and soft gasps.

I replied, "I'm from the border planet, Chuck. I was born and raised there."

He slumped, disgusted: Urrea scores a kung-fu blow of his own.

Later, he took revenge in Bend, Oregon. We were on a panel with Ursula K. Le Guin and other writers, talking about the future of the American West. I was in the middle of speaking my piece, preaching border glasnost, when Bowden simply sighed into his microphone and groaned, "Oh, God."

Then he went outside to smoke.

III

Once I moved to Tucson, we drifted apart a little. Chuck had become addicted to the ongoing drug war. He had gone from damaging his soul on the southern Arizona immigrant killing fields to feeding on terror and blood with the crime photographers of Juarez. He was wandering in West Texas and southern

New Mexico. Rumors of his demise proliferated. His foes and competitors were predicting his fall—surely, Bowden couldn't keep it up.

When he was in town, we spoke. I knew he was a gardener, and had a rumored backyard wonderland. But it felt indecorous to invite myself over to his place, even when he said I should.

Chuck railed against what he called the "Dead Ed Industry." He was drawn to evil and corpses and bad mojo and worse governments, sure. But I am convinced that the Dead Ed freaks had a hand in making him flee Tucson. I had seen the pain he hid with bravado. How does such a person show that he is vulnerable?

He complained that people who had once drunk a beer in the same cantina as Ed were now claiming to be his best friends, and were offering to take people to Ed's unlawful burial spot somewhere out there near the Devil's Highway. "They could just show suckers a pile of rocks in the backyard and say 'This is Edward Abbey's secret grave,' and they'd believe it." He was furious.

This was when Chuck told me Ed's Red Caddy was moldering away in a dirt alley behind Speedway, the street where we had first met.

"It's covered in raccoon shit," he noted.

Fellow Tucson writer Gregory McNamee confirmed this story. It seemed like some urban legend. If Ed was such a titan, how was his car left out in the dirt? So Greg drove me down the alley one night, and there it was. A well-known book dealer had acquired it. It had become something of a shrine to certain writers, who ogled it and wrote WASH ME in its dust and drank beer in Ed's honor. It became my habit to visit the car often. I didn't ever tell Chuck, though.

Tony Delcavo, of Bella Luna Books in Colorado, bought the old car. He invited me to help drive it to Denver. That amusing semi-epic journey became an essay called "Down the High-way with Edward Abbey." McNamee kindly published it in an Abbey-themed anthology. And here I am, mourning Chuck in print. What a circle.

Charles Bowden. I consider him a master—if not in every book or utterance, certainly a master of audacity. He fought to maintain his integrity. He always tried to tell the truth, even when he lied. Chuck knew things, terrible and beautiful things. I feel richer for reading him and knowing him.

If you listen, you will hear him from the other side, saying "Oh, God" when I say I loved him.

As he wrote about Abbey:

In some way I can't quite put my finger on, he's not quite dead.

L.A.U.
Chicago
2017

drive, he said

HOLD HARMLESS AGREEMENT:
warning, vehicle *not* equipped
with seat belts or air bags

I don't bring a lot to the table. I knew him, we were friends and we had a lot of good talk. But there were no big moments, dramatic events, or secret missions. There is no cache of letters. I'd pretty much pitch those as they came in. I was trained up as a historian but apparently the training never took. I am by nature a person who takes things as they come and that is how I took him. The only thing special about him to me was our friendship, since I don't make friends with everyone I meet.

Now I run into people who are struck that I knew him and I always tell them it was not a very hard thing to do. He was reasonably polite, didn't shit on the floor, and was well read. This last point mattered to me since I devour books, and like most such wretches love to talk about what I have read and even better argue about it. He had a similar pathology. I admired what he wrote and by and large agreed with it—not just philosophically, but viscerally. I suspect I was born already knowing a lot of what is in his books, it seems to come with a certain ornery cracker territory as part of the blood. So, naturally, we never wasted time on such commonplaces but talked about other things.

I have never kept a diary or journal. I really don't keep anything but memories. So, I cannot dip into the awesome details
of some day or night. This is okay, because nothing was really
awesome anyway. That kind of significance seems to be cus-
tomarily applied like gold gilt by death. At least, that is the
sense I get from listening to people talk about him and reading
what they write about him. I do not share the feeling. I think
this translation into desert sage, Western god, or whatever is a
diminishment of both him and his words. He was a man born
to strangle gurus with their own entrails and everything he
ever thought or did is pointless if he is suddenly indispens-
able and irreplaceable. There is a lot of cheap talk nowadays
that uses strange, ugly-sounding words like empowerment, as
if power can be given to someone. He didn't think that. He
thought we could all take power and be free, and spent a lot
time writing essays and novels explaining just how to do such a
thing. In a real sense if he did his job right someday we'll stop
reading him because we will have taken him at his word and
broken out of our industrial cage and moved on to dangerous
and liberating ground. I would love to live in a nation where
no one read him because everyone already knew what he had
to say and had acted on it. Things are looking up, but I think
it'll still be a while before I get my wish.

There is a clutter to life that ideas can never tolerate or make
go away. To unravel something, you have to have a thesis. But
to understand the dead ends, back alleys, and side roads of life
itself, you have to mistrust your thesis and constantly keep an
eye on it lest it blind you to detail, contradiction, lust, love,
and loneliness. I can't write about a friend and make it neat and
tidy unless I intend to kill my friend. And this is not my inten-
tion. To be an expert on someone you know, I truly believe,
is never to have known them at all. Which is why we assign

such work to scholars. We say they will be objective, while we ourselves cannot promise such a feat. But we also think they can be certain, while we cannot comprehend such a fantasy. To really know someone, to break bread with them and talk and drink and laugh and argue, is much like knowing an ecosystem. You can get the drift, draw a map, know many trails, but the more you know the more convinced you become that absolute knowing is impossible.

I am not trying to make life or a life mystifying. I am just not willing to lie about the vast reefs and grottos that lurk beneath the waters, the geography of the deep that we can never see and concerning which we seldom receive reports. Once in a great while a whale is beached and at dawn as the light comes on we all rush to the shore, clamber about the leviathan and for the briefest moment convince ourselves we now have a sense of the life that transpires in the great depths where light never penetrates. We touch the hoary skin of the beast and examine with silent horror the strange scars that rake the body. We imagine the power hidden in the torso and stare into the great eyes, each the size of a hubcap, and think we can catch a last flicker of what they saw and of the torrent of life that poured through the big lens into the hidden life of the mind now locked within the colossal skull.

It is late afternoon, the light has gone from white toward gold and the fresh coolness of fall grows stronger each day. He is coming up the sidewalk to the library, the gait slow but not clumsy. There is no need for speed, and his limbs swing with fluid grace. The eyes are clear, and a faint smile rides easy on the face. We sit on a ledge near a statue of some nymph. His shirt is worn but the tears are neatly stitched and the jeans look pressed. The vest completes the costume. He waves a sheaf of papers at me, the manuscript of a book, or what I think is a book, that I have just scribbled. It's publishable, he says, I'll help you find a publisher. You think so?

Yes. We are in a strange geography, the place not yet fixed on any map—the imaginary world created by words on paper. But we do not talk about this. To talk too much is a taboo and we both know this fact, it is something we will never discuss. The existence of the taboo is a given, we are of the same culture. To talk of these matters is to kill them and destroy what little magic is possible. We both know the killers will come soon enough. For both of us, writing is too important to merit discussion. We sit there for five or ten minutes talking softly as the light grows more and more golden. We are strangers with a third typewritten stranger between us. There is a limit to our knowing, even if we are friends, even if the book is now common knowledge between us. Screams, small cries, sighs, and shouts come off the heap of pages he holds and we can hear them faintly as we talk to each other, sitting on the ledge as college students float past. His eyes keep scanning coeds, his voice never rises. He gets out a pen, gives me names, and he says, call them or write them and use my name. I say thanks. He shrugs.

We both stand and go our separate ways. The ledge is a beach, and without a word or a look back we both enter our own waters and vanish beneath the waves. That is the knowing we are always left with, and that is also, of course, the lack of knowing. It is why I cannot write with the certainty of the scholars or the critics or the various police agencies. It is also why I am able to write about a red Cadillac and have no doubt about the machine's performance or the driver's skills and quirks. Because I am not an expert, I am not the final authority, but I am a witness to the ride and I have felt the wind against my face on those good days when the top is down and life is up . . .

My hands are cold, the mornings are beginning to whisper winter and I'm thinking firewood, good books, and a drink in the hand as the flames leap and the coals fall glowing through the grate. There will be pork roasts, long nights, and skim ice at first light. Life's a pretty good thing if you are willing to chew on it and swallow. I remember standing in a parking lot with him a week or two before he died and he's insisting on signing one of his books for me and I'm fighting the idea. I point out that his name is already printed on the title page, the book jacket, and the book spine but he dismisses my simple logic with an indifferent wave of his hand. The sun streams down as he bends over and scribbles some necessary bullshit in the book and then hands me a copy of *The Fool's Progress*. Shit, I say, I already bought a copy. What am I supposed to do with this one? He shrugs with a kindly fuck-you expression and then drives off. The day he dies I pull the novel off the shelf and for the first time read his scrawl—"fellow traveler in this fool's journey out of the dark, through the light, and into the unknown. . . ." Okay, I'll take him at his word.

There is the matter of the plastic shrink wrap. It's lying about a foot away as I write, covering a tidy rectangle of cardboard encasing a videotape. His face is glowering on the cover— what is this shit? I never saw him glower. More stancing, ass-hole?—and the title clangs out "a voice in the wilderness." Well, la-de-dah. He looks like a rusty hatchet, he's got this western cowboy bonnet on his noggin, a red bandanna—Jesus Christ! Do you have no shame, man?—and his piercing eyes say I'm the one, bubba. Bullshit. Anyway, inside the box cowering under plastic wrap is a one-hour documentary that I have never watched. It's been out six months, a year, I can't remember. I glance at the jacket copy—"a writer in the mold of Twain and Thoreau . . . a larger-than-life figure as big as the West itself." What? I remember the day the crew of two arrived, shuffling into my hut with tripod and stout camera boxes. I was deranged then with a book about a savings and loan wizard and their descent was a bit of a jolt. They sniffed about my ruins and finally picked a location in the backyard where I slumped in a chair and the camera ate a big mesquite, some cactus and a dash of salvia and chuperosa. The director asked questions. I gave answers. And then they left.

A lot of my friends have seen the show and told me it is good. I liked the director and the camera guy. But I have never watched it. Never opened it, for that matter. It lies over there like a Pandora's box—sorry, honey, I think we'll just keep the lid on for the moment. I've got a good idea what is on the tape from the endless précis friends have offered up. I remember nothing that I said, but that is not a problem. I am used to seeing myself on screens and conditioned to the ghastly image, so that is not it. True, I do not own a television or VCR but I know kindly folk who do, so that is not what is stopping me. But I cannot watch it. I'm not ready. I just thought you should know this fact. There is some unfinished business in my gut. You want objective, turn on the set. I do not know the country.

We'll skip the fame game questions, like now that he's dead just how does he measure up? They're a waste of time since they eventually will answer themselves. He put out twenty books or so, they sold here and there and when he died *Time* magazine gave him an obit. On the other hand, I had a strange conversation a while back with a Washington columnist. He called me up all excited and told me he had his FBI file, the whole damn thing. I said that's interesting, and allowed how I'd known the guy. He said, really? this is incredible, and went on and on about the weird coincidences possible in this best of all possible worlds. We rattled on for about twenty minutes before I realized he was talking about Abbie Hoffman. I said, no, no, the other guy. What other guy, he asked? When I explained, it turned out he'd never heard of him. Well, that's fame for you and a demonstration of the power and reach of *Time* magazine.

Still I run into strange-looking people from time to time who seem to memorize his words like scripture. I find this unsettling but harmless. There is even a calendar out that gives you a dose of his wisdom every day. A fellow once told me he was in a laundromat up in the plateau country with grimy backpackers and they were all hunched over reading him while their clothes twirled and soaked. The fame stuff, as I said, will take care of itself. The measuring for a literary winding sheet is best left to the trolls of the Academy who camp near the fabled canon and guard it with their lives and footnotes. In due time they'll get the job done and crank out the appropriate texts like canned Spam. We'll just have to wait until they reveal to us what he really meant and whether any of it was truly up to snuff.

In some way I can't quite put my finger on, he's not quite dead. Death is not as simple as the doctors like to make it out to be. I'm around people all the time who are clinically alive and yet actually dead. This morning I stopped in to see how an old man I know was doing. He is a feisty guy, has about seventy-five years, and lately has had a run of bad luck. First came the stroke, then when the ambulance got him to the hospital, he had, as I recall, a cardiac episode. Pneumonia weighed in right after that. And then the DT's hit bad. The old man, a grizzled cracker and a killer, had a daily thirst that ran somewhere between a case and a case and a half of beer. Now, as a crowning touch, cancer has arrived and he's about to ship out to the hospital for a twice-daily six-week bombardment of radiation. His string is about run out.

Anyway, I'm in this living room where the old man is staying—a friendly couple has taken him in in his sickness. He's sitting on the couch, his aluminum walker standing in front of him. The woman is on his one side, her husband is on the other, and the old man is smoking one of his hand-rolled cigarettes. He is very quiet, he feels that bony hand on his shoulder and I can see this fact in his vacant eyes. Naked women writhe from the tattoos on his withered arms. Around his ankles are scars from that long-ago southern chain gang. What strikes me is the way the woman and her husband are talking about the old man, about his health, the upcoming radiation therapy, his cancer, his doctors, the whole medical shebang. They are talking right through him. He no longer exists. Their words are like x-rays passing through his flesh. His eyes register no complaint about this fact. He knows that he is already dead.

When I leave, the husband walks me out to my truck. He says, "You know, what surprised me is he never asked for his gun. I thought he would." I tell him that will never happen, it's not the way the old man was trained to play things out. I tell him the old man simply does not know how to die, only how to live, and because of this fact he will have to live until he dies and damn the pain. I don't mention that he considers himself already dead and that the man and his wife talk of him as if he were already dead. I think it all comes down to what you drive. The old man waiting on the couch for his heart to stop beating lacks the right machine. He does not possess a Cadillac. He cannot conjure up a dream. I do not think he has ever been able to dream.

Dreamers make the best drivers, always. They are not afraid of unknown routes, they do not complain about bumps in the road, and they like the feel of the machine roaring down the dark highways. They seldom if ever get lost because wherever they find themselves is part of what they were seeking.

Meanwhile, it's drive time.

The chariot is a 1975 Cadillac Eldorado convertible, color red. He bought it for himself as his sixtieth birthday present. It had an old eight-track tape system and he was so thrilled by this device he raced out and bought a stack of old eight-tracks. But the tape player never worked. When a friend admired it, he told the guy he'd paid $4500 for it. Not true. He'd plunked down six grand for this behemoth that got about eight miles to the gallon and needed a new rag top. Did it without warning, too—forgot to tell the wife, you know. Had to have it. I guess he felt a deep need for this veritable icon of greed, shallow taste and industrialism. Disgraced himself, once again. And then when a network news show wanted him to return to the haunts of one of his best-known books, why by God he showed up in this obscene automobile and by hook or by crook made the caddy a key character in his offhanded denunciation of the twentieth century and a lot of other stuff.

Let's get in the caddy and cruise. Runs fine, so don't worry, although the exhaust system is pretty loud. The trunk's loaded with tools—nails, dynamite, sand, wire cutters, a .30-30 Model

94 and a fine set of monkey wrenches. The night's fine, the tank's full. Open the ice chest and crack a cold one. Let's roll.

cruise control setting

I don't believe in doing work I don't want to do in order to live the way I don't want to live.

Edward Abbey, *The Fool's Progress: An Honest Novel*

After midnight the cops coop along the interstate, hunker in the dip separating the lanes, roll down their windows and, looking like couples doing a 69, talk shop as their police radios crackle. They're bored, but then they usually are, and half-watch the traffic looking for the drunk who's bobbing and weaving in a show-off manner or the speed freak who's flaunting the rules of safety and fuel conservation. It's a hot night and as the police grumble to each other about the fucking captain and the old lady and their second job as a rent-a-cop, bats feed quietly above their heads and snakes slide under the chassis of their vehicles seeking a comely rat. Suddenly a pair of headlights comes barreling down the pike, devouring the distance at a frightening rate. The cops grow quiet. One aims the cannon of his radar and shouts with joy when his machine clocks one hundred and ten. The enemy nears and instantly flashes by, an old ragtop red Cadillac with the roof down and some fool catatonic behind the wheel, his beard flapping in the wind like a scarf. The officers fire up, hit the lights, and spin their tires off the dirt and onto the warm pavement as they leap hungrily into a satisfying hot pursuit. They never catch up with the caddy and their radio calls ahead to other safety goons fail to verify a sighting. The damn red beast just disappears.

The wild bird store sells no wild birds. The blues stroke the air and hundreds of feeders for cardinals, hummingbirds, orioles, finches, squirrels, woodpeckers and other creatures dangle from racks. I am trying not to think. In an hour or two, I'm to be the moderator on a panel—fifth anniversary of his death. What did he used to claim? That the only birds he could identify were fried chicken and the rosy-bottomed skinny dipper? An absolute lie, of course. I can remember walking along an arroyo with him one morning, the air cool under the trees, the sun warm on my face, and birds darting here and there in the brush as he ticked them off like a rosary. We weren't carrying binoculars or guide books, we were not doing much of anything beyond ambling and talking and not talking—a morning kind of work. His head was kind of hunkered down as if he were considering the possibility of a big idea flashing across his mind, and he certainly looked the part with his full head of graying hair, his bristling Old Testament beard, a face that looked chiseled out of hard rock, keenly focused blue eyes, a good-sized nose riding ahead like an ax, and that low rumbling monotone of a voice. Basically, the crazed, lice-ridden, raving, pedestal-sitting anchorite sage from central casting with spittle on his lips and flames shooting out his mouth—until his lusty gaze alights on a pretty girl and the wicked bastard beckons for her to hop into his red Cadillac convertible. Not a pretty boy, but handsome is as handsome does.

The naming is a compulsive human act—we can name something, it exists and therefore we exist. I know I'm subject to this naming fetish. A tree doesn't really exist to me until I can mumble out loud its species. People have to be filed in tidy groups, fascists or communists or Democrats or Republicans or suckers for the Le Leche league. In the beginning was the word and the word was. . . . None of us seems able to stop this labeling fetish, certainly not me. But I know this seeming necessity for our cortex is in some part a crime against truth and life itself. So I dread the program I am to moderate and the ceaseless naming that will ensue. People who knew him will be on the panel, and they'll tell stories about him, or explain him or in some way name him. I hate this business and for the better part of the year have tried to get out of it. I anticipate the categories, claims, charges, churlish epithets all swirling around the room and seeping like poison gas into the lives of a couple hundred people who have come out for the show. What the hell did he say? Something like I am a humanist, I'd sooner kill a man than a snake?

As I write this early in the morning my eyes lift from the computer screen and I see the flash of a peregrine falcon as it wheels off my bird feeder twenty feet away. This is the second one in a month. I live in the center of a city of 700,000 people—Jesus Christ! Boom! a dove hits the window, the falcon is back. Suddenly my rational world crumbles and the deep sense of superstition that broods within me wells up. The peregrine is an omen, the omen is good, and I know this absolutely. The bird is also a killer dining on, among other things, domestic pigeons and poultry, grebes, auklets, murrelets, small gulls, terns, petrels, wild ducks, small shearwaters, small herons, coots, gallinules, rails, woodcock, snipe, sandpipers, plovers, quail, grouse, ptarmigans, pheasants, sparrow hawks, cuckoos, kingfishers, mourning doves, flickers and other woodpeckers, marsh hawks, whippoorwills, nighthawks, swifts, kingbirds, jays, crows, phoebes, starlings, bobolinks, blackbirds, orioles, grackles, meadowlarks, swallows, warblers, robins—well, you get the idea. They also have acrobatic mating customs that seem to us exhibitionist. They tend to live on cliffs with good views and are what we might call horizon types. Damn near died out during the DDT binge after the second war when there no longer seemed to be a place for them among our crowd. Now they are back, diving in my yard, terrifying the songbirds and putting a talon in my eye.

Ten, twenty, thirty thousand years of human evolution vanish and I am ready to enter a cave and begin smearing paints as I seek to capture the power of the beasts, my brothers and sisters. Of course, there are technical points to resolve. He always planned to come back as a vulture, even used to make drawings of himself in this elevated state, but now he may have opted to be a peregrine. Then again, he did fib quite a bit. And peregrines are meat eaters, and I can't imagine him letting anything cross his beak without a good dollop of cholesterol in it. I am relieved in part because my tortoise, Lightning, hasn't staggered past for about a week. Tortoises were another one of his fantasy creatures, in fact up until the murderous dives by the peregrine, I'd assumed tortoises were his last fantasy.

The wild bird store is a great comfort, with its tidy bins full of black sunflower, striped sunflower, hemp, safflower, and millet seed, its buckets of groundup bugs, its packets of hummingbird food, its nice bars of fruit for orioles, the twenty-pound blocks for quail and the upright piano in the back room with sheet music for ragtime. Sometimes after closing hour we all go into the back room and have a joint while old blues singers wail and the water cascades down the rocks into the bird pond. There is not a scrap of him in this store, there almost never is in these places. He is still too dangerous. AIDS? Herd all the patients out into the desert and leave them to die before they fuck up our sex lives. Illegal immigration? Stop those Mexicans at the border, give 'em each a Winchester 94 and a case of ammo, and then send them home equipped to solve their own problems. Industrial civilization? Kill it before it kills you. Blow up the goddamn dams, bum the bulldozers, shoot the cattle, put alligators in the stock ponds. And never ever trust the state. Anarchism, my friend. Hispanic culture? Hopelessly anti-nature, anti-democratic. Got to keep an eye on them or they'll corrupt what little we've retained from Bunker Hill, the Green Mountain Boys, Billie Holiday and Charles Ives. And by the way, honey, bring that bottle over here and loosen up.

I look at the Audubon bird prints on the wall and the hummingbird earrings in the case and know there is no way to cleanly integrate him into here. Sorry, knowing and loving birds is not enough. He used to give ten percent of his income—which as a rule didn't amount to much—to causes, and then some of the recipients would become outraged by what he wrote. Terms like eco-pornography would be tossed around like brickbats and he'd get all indignant at the charges. I tell you, it was always a mess. Once, a bunch of Mexican-Americans threatened to picket my magazine office because of one of his verbal hand grenades denouncing patronism and nagging about a Latin tendency to see nature as a utility device, not a soul-saving wilderness—I can still hear the grandmotherly voice of the woman on the phone asking, "Why would he write something so hurtful?" I didn't tell her the truth: that he probably didn't know himself why he wrote it.

I turn my attention to the tubs of ground-up-bugs—a local product whipped up by a woman after her day job. I know he'd like them, I certainly do. One of my delights is smearing this gunk on feeders as my come-on to woodpeckers and flycatchers. I keep it in the refrigerator by the steam beer. I've got a special feeder with plexiglass sides so that I can see the long, lascivious tongues of the woodpeckers as they have at it. I'm sure I could have sold him on feeding woodpeckers.

Time to go. I shuffle toward the door of the air-conditioned-strip-commercial-shopping-plaza store, a box uglier than any sin I know and now a bastion of nature. I love this store but I can't deny the heat of the asphalt tundra that spreads like lava around it. People come here to buy tokens, clues, passports, symbols, gestures, icons, and prayers to a wild and free world. But they can't buy him here or any of his kind. He doesn't fit. He is not a feeder boy, I guess.

Out the door, in the glare and warp of midday heat rising from the concrete and asphalt floor of this edition of the living desert, through the brown air of dust and machine fumes, under the white sun torching through the atmosphere and licking our skin with love and leaving cancerous hickeys, somewhere out there the red caddy is at idle, anxious to go pedal-to-the-metal. The roof is down, the miles per gallon a disgrace, the seats soft, the ashtray generous, the factory air monstrous, the function unclear. Like love, the red caddy has its own reasons.

It is the car we all wish to drive. But of course we all can't. His car, you know. And ragtops, no matter how many airbags, seat belts, roll bars and insurance policies we freight them with, can never be made safe. Took out Isadora Duncan when her scarf got caught in the spokes of a wheel, decapitated Jayne Mansfield, sprayed John Kennedy's brains all over his wife. Just when you start to relax they might haul off and hurt you. Can't be sure of them until they go to the junkyard and even then it's best to see them crushed into a tidy metal bale. Otherwise, there is always the possibility of an accident.

I drive toward the looming program down Speedway, the main drag of my town and a national whipping boy in the ugliness derby. For decades it has been the American touchstone for bad taste—*Life* magazine once touted it in a photograph as a world-class eyesore and since then the jackals of the media have returned to the street for its abundant carrion. I love Speedway down to its nice tacky name. At night kids cruising roll up and down it, drunks bob and weave through the traffic, punks park and sit on the hoods of their trucks and do a hardball scowl, carloads of adolescent girls ripple past giggling over the notions of sex and cleavage.

Long ago, I fell into this world. There was a march by angry women to protest the rape and mayhem they faced daily after the sun went down. They called this demonstration Take Back the Night. Naturally, they stomped up Speedway because it seemed a distillate of the menace they were denouncing. People lined the street watching this surly parade. Afterward, they found a seven-year-old girl in a passageway between two homely strip commercial buildings. She was dead, eviscerated. I was starting out as a reporter and my publisher and editor shipped me off into the world of permanent night. I'm not sure I ever came back completely.

I whip past the belt of biker bars and joints offering topless dancers, private booths with women sitting behind a barrier buck naked while the customer masturbates, adult book stores, the whole arsenal of the American flesh trade. I've never been in an adult bookstore. He loved this belt. Once he took his aged father to a porn movie palace and the old man was reportedly horrified. Another time he was said to have taken an adolescent girl to one of the joints as some kind of prelude to what would soon become their marriage. He was big on biodiversity.

Speedway always means life and life is always a wonderful thing, but not necessarily pretty.

At one intersection, my town issued its first speeding ticket in the early days of this century—to a rich boy on a tear, naturally. The town's first modern serial killer used to wander Speedway like a Pied Piper. I went to high school with him. When they finally stuffed him into the joint for a long good-bye he became a poet. Then another con killed him.

I try to create order in my mind for the looming program— gotta be serious. The event will be held in a very distinguished hotel before a very proper audience. I feel like I'm being asked to introduce a badass rap singer to a herd of seminary students. He said, "Liberty is life: *eros* plus *anarchos* equals *bios*." He said, "If there is anyone here I've failed to insult, I apologize." Of course, in the five years since he died, he's cleaned up his act. No one talks much about a lot of things he said or why he said them. That's why the panel discussion is going to take place: he is dead and since he is dead, he is safe. Somehow they've slipped a giant condom around his life's work.

I park a half block from the hotel—always plan your escape route. And wander into the old pink building, a living fossil built by the heiress to a copper fortune around 1930 to provide genteel lodgings for genteel people in this Mexican hellhole of a town burning in this unspeakable desert. The grounds are neatly landscaped and everything hides behind big hedges. The Duke and Duchess of Windsor used to stay here when they were mooching in this part of the world. Howard Hughes booked a suite here for a couple decades but never showed up. The old building is like a maiden aunt. The food is fair to terrible, the rugs have a ratty feel but seem redeemed by that aura of high-class wear and tear. I like the bar, a deadly pub with scattered couches and huge Audubon prints from the old man's work on quadrupeds, that unfinished poem he was painting before senility nailed his lively mind and lusty soul. As I enter this booze parlor it is as quiet as a church except for a low sound off to my side. I look over and see a friend of mine, a political bagman and real estate wheeler-dealer. He's sitting at a table with a couple of suits and doubtless is engineering the murder of some new tract of desert in order to finance his recurring holidays on the coast. He pretends I do not exist. It is apparently not the moment to admit he knows my ilk.

I order a coffee and fall back into my dour mood. I feel some kind of . . . guilt? sin? I can't put my finger on it. They want to know what can be known but they do not want to know what can't be known. They want anecdotes, little intimacies, clues to habits and dress, pieces of the True Beer Can or True Old Pickup Truck. But they do not want to know who he really was, that core part each of us carries that others can only guess at and never really comprehend or possess—that we ourselves cannot fully understand. The most important part of a person remains unknown even to the person, the fire that from time to time causes a life to become a conflagration. Where the light comes from and why.

Why this book? And after that, why that book? Why the books at all? Why all this effort and pain? That is the part we seldom if ever get to know about ourselves. We are usually afraid to ask, but should we be of unusual courage, our questioning will normally avail us very little. It is much easier to find out who someone slept with than to discover what animated their waking hours and rode roughshod through the dreams that filled their nights. Such things almost always remain mysteries for a very simple reason. We do not know in any very convincing fashion why we are alive or why life itself exists. It is a great liberty granted us in a dark universe and we take this liberty without many questions and live it and then die while remaining as profoundly ignorant of the forces we embody as when we were babes in arms. He once wrote that he had never heard a mountain lion bawling about its fate and I always liked that statement. But I am not a mountain lion.

I am a person who lives in a world I can at times explain but seldom, if ever, understand. But I am here now, ready for the program. I have the experience and skill to recount things that happen in an orderly manner. Take a killing, one that happened in my world. Yukon Bob and Be-Bop drank all day in the gypsy bar, got real drunk and stupid. This was not unusual. They got drunk pretty much all the time. Small-town America is a boring place for most small-town Americans. I will describe the air outside: hot, dry, the light blinding, and always the dust, faint brown dust floating in the air and coating your tongue. This air of the desert sounds unappealing and yet when swallowed even for a very short while becomes a lifelong addiction. He would understand this, as he would the all-day drinking bout. He was of this place, more or less, and of this blood. He knew the lost people and their fate.

The gypsy bar has a different air, a fetid, smoky, urine-soaked quality. It combines the worst elements of a mine shaft, a bathroom and a train station. Nothing in this old saloon feels clean or ever will. Even the green felt on the pool table looks very tired. Finally, Yukon Bob and Be-Bop are cast out of the saloon. They go to a friend's house with some other people and continue their drinking. The land here, I suspect, is simply too large for many people and in their fear the drink becomes essential. Hours after night falls, the two men continue a quarrel they had begun in the saloon: who gets to fuck the girl. Nobody really knows the girl's name and if you ask, they just say, you know, the fat one. Finally, the two men go for a ride and the following afternoon Be-Bop is found dead in a wash by a local party animal named Shuffle Skull. The police look at the corpse and say, "DRT," Dead Right There. Terms are always our safety belts in life.

Yukon Bob and three other men who took part in the drinking voluntarily go to the police to help them in their investigation. After hearing them out, the cops bust Yukon Bob and we will not likely see him again for a long time, if ever. We will know the answer for the killing. It was over a girl, you know, and then we will move on with our lives. Yukon Bob will rot in prison and Be-Bop will rot in the ground and I suspect both of them in their booze-fogged memories will rest content with this explanation of a night gone bad. But I never will because I will never really understand why it happened. I will just know how to tell the story and keep the sequence right. But this is not life and if we forget this fact, we give up all hope of understanding the few clues that might ever come our way.

Why did he write this book? And the book after that? Why did he write at all?

I just know I don't want to do this program. For a year, I've refused, whined, wheedled, done everything I know to get out of it. I have frankly been browbeaten, outmaneuvered, and cowed. I am here. Somehow I always thought the day would never arrive. I was wrong, a recurrent event in my life. The quiet tasteful room slowly stokes the anger within me, a cheap, easily dismissed anger that despises good taste as a mask behind which to hide the horrors that seem to dance before my eyes. I can feel flames creep up my throat and if this fire reaches my tongue we are all in for a world of hurt. Years ago,

I sloshed through a boozy evening in this room with a writer who had flown in to profile him. The guy was clean-cut, living somewhere up in the Rockies, feeding on Bombay Gin, and polishing his first novel. He'd been a tennis pro and now had put down the racket and picked up the pen. He was a smart guy with a quick and critical intelligence. He'd been out to the house interviewing him, and then down to the university archive going through his papers. And by the time I showed up to be interviewed, he was mad.

So for hours we guzzled and talked. All in all, a pleasant evening of barbed words and good cheer on his abundant expense account. He had a simple kind of thesis: he felt his subject was a mean fake. I didn't agree but I come from a culture where you tolerate opinions and refuse to indulge in cheap concepts like heresy. It was the correspondence he read down at the archive that finally put him over the edge. The letters were witty, brilliant, vicious, and often enraged. They were apparently full of denunciations of critics, of other writers, of the planet in general, and of the literary moguls that seemingly run the lit biz. The writer was really pissed at my friend's crusade against Henry James the Dead and John Updike the Living. He explained that these attacks—apparently he spent hours reading epistles that cast both these worthies into the inner circle of hell or the shower room of a serious prison—came from my friend's sense of inadequacy, his innate evil spirit, and his puerile jealousy. I mildly disagreed and only added that such exercises seemed a waste of time to me but if they made someone feel better, what the hell, it was okay by me. I'd had these conversations with my friend on many occasions and gleefully shared his sentiments but lacked his enthusiasm for expressing them.

Then we waded into the inevitable thesis, one I'd been waiting for like a toad on a fly trail, that I was to be the successor.

Here, I indulged in a bit of mock anger, merely noting that we hardly needed a new model since the classic model was still operating so well that he could drive a professional profiler into a tizzy and force him to imbibe serious amounts of gin in a sedate bar surrounded by Audubon's shrouds of vanishing or vanished fauna.

I didn't bother to tell him the obvious: nobody needed a new model because now there were thousands, maybe tens of thousands of chips off the old, wrathy block. Pull into any gas station and you'll find him there. Sometimes he will be young, sometimes old, sometimes a man, sometimes a woman. He'll cross class lines, do damn near any kind of work, often look just like everyone else, and be crazy as a shithouse rat. He'll tell you his name is Jim or Jane and seem perfectly normal then somehow it becomes apparent she thinks a bug is as important as a Homo sapiens or that a rock pile is just fine and nope, not interested in selling no matter what the price. The word wilderness will slip out, and dynamite, sand in the crankcase, slow elk, naked swimming mixed with William Blake and have a beer, bub. She'll drink herbal tea and while she sips out of a fine china cup she'll explain that a coyote's fangs around a lamb's throat is not an unpleasant prospect. New model? He's become a consciousness and she is everywhere.

Once, I was in a national park office and noticed the book racks had none of his works. I asked a ranger why. He looked at me for a second and then snapped, "Because my fucking superintendent won't let me stock them." So there you have it—sometimes he even masquerades as a ranger with that natty uniform and comical hat. So it goes like that, everything seems fine and on the level and then she sees, say, a new subdivision and land scraped bare, and her mouth snarls and you hear her muttering, "Nunca mas, never again."

When the profile surfaced some months later it was as I had suspected: a quick retrospective of the career, then a zoom lens and lots of videotape on The Problem, an early coda of me denouncing the notion of being a successor (I knew my mock anger would pass muster as indignation and heartfelt feeling), and then a fade-out about an overrated reputation fueled by an overweening ego. Spell the name right, it'll sell the books— that was my final take on the piece. What it never mentioned was the real source of my gin-swilling companion's rage: his subject was an original, and my drinking buddy that night knew he wasn't and he never would be.

Suddenly, a proper woman dressed like a defrocked nun tugs at my elbow and I look up into her herbal-tea face. She is clutching one of his books and she explains that there will be an auction and would I pick a selection for her to read to the audience before the bidding begins? I flip open the volume and instantly go to a single paragraph. I say, "Read this to THEM." I see the look in her eye and think maybe I should have a nice eleven a.m. drink. Maybe a quick hit will befuddle me enough to quench this burning in me. But then I reconsider. These morning belts have a history of backfiring.

She thanks me politely and goes off with the passage:

> . . . That's all I ask of the author. To be a hero, appoint
> himself a moral leader, wanted or not. I believe that words
> count, that writing matters, that poems, essays, and nov-
> els—in the long run—make a difference. If they do not,
> then in the words of my exemplar Aleksandr Solzhenitsyn,
> ". . . . the writer's work is of no more importance than the
> barking of village dogs at night." The hack writer, the

temporizer, the toady, and the sycophant, the journalistic
courtier (and what is a courtier but a male courtesan?), all
those in the word trade who simply go with the flow, who
never oppose the rich and powerful, are no better in my
view than Solzhenitsyn's village dogs. The dogs bark: the
caravan moves on.

I have always liked that paragraph because it sums up one
of the things that made him different: he thought words and
acts should connect. It is not enough to describe the world,
you have got to change it. His hands-on bias started very early
I suspect.

Once I came off a mountain in the Sierra Madre and when
I finally got down to the dirt road I was hot and tired and my
pack was stuffed with orchid specimens. To my surprise, I
found a couple parked in a VW van. They were Americans, but
I forgave them this fact when the guy said howdy and handed
me a cold beer. Seems they were going to wander Mexico for a
couple of months with no real agenda. The guy had just made
a killing up in Oregon by designing some newfangled bird
feeders. We got to talking about nothing in particular and he
asked if I knew of this writer who preached monkey wrenching and the like. I didn't respond and he kept right on rolling
anyway. He explained how he and the writer had attended the
University of New Mexico back in the early fifties and how
they'd roared around at night and taken out billboards. Ini-
tially, they cut them down, he explained, and then when the
sign people switched to steel posts and concrete, they'd esca-
lated to dynamite. I kind of chuckled softly to myself about the
research techniques of the American novelist. I never saw the
guy again, and after all those beers I can't remember his name.
But I suspect there are fewer signs in Mexico now.

Ah, time for my medicine show to move on. I can hear the rustling of the arriving audience in the lobby. My friend is still making his pitch to the suits at the window overlooking the patio. And he is still pretending I do not exist, a sound business decision, in my opinion. I inventory the corpus delecti. I've just come up from the ranch, a hideaway four or five miles from the Mexican line where in the morning the birds flock to my feeders and then the falcons come to kill the dumb seed-eating birds. Coyotes gobble the cottontails that shiver on my doorstep, and owls run the midnight shift of slaughter. I can't see an electric light in my valley and I'm careful where I step because of the cowshit. Beulah, my trusty rattlesnake, guards the east door, javelinas root hell out of everything and a lion is working the territory. There is no phone and the mail never comes. The gate is locked, the house hidden from view.

At night I hear the soft purring of drug caravans beating a path to the hungry and empty cities. Choppers and fixed-wings regularly hunt the land and the salvia and chuperosa are growing with a rush as the days lengthen. Down at the ranch, I keep calm.

And the damnedest thing is I sometimes catch a glimpse of him crashing through the mesquite bosque or trudging up toward the oaks. He's always playing that recorder—and not too well—like some shit-kicking Pan.

This goes with the territory. I live on seriously haunted ground and since settlement days everyone has been trying to deny or denounce this fact. For openers, the Native Americans are still here, tens of thousands of them, and they take up a lot of space. We've also got skinwalkers, *brujas*, *curanderas*, witches, and a few serial killers. The earth here is dotted with ruins and from time to time you can feel the bony hands of the dead on your shoulders. There are strange voices in the night and once a Mexican American woman took me to the side street where she'd bumped into the Virgin of Guadalupe one evening. Industrialism may be killing my place but somehow it has never really taken root. Nobody believes in it, not even the bankers. The land always overwhelms our little workshops and power plants and licks at the sides of our buildings. We touch the marble walls and briefly feel reassured but in some deep part of us lurks a permanent dread. We wake up with night sweats and wonder if the dunes are marching and burying our world. We do things by the numbers out here, but secretly suspect some magic is afoot that will overwhelm all our equations.

When the Europeans first started cruising my desert looking for gold and souls, they bumped up against some Indians who seemed to already have a grip on the Jesuits' tales of God. Juan Matheo Manje, a Spanish soldier, left an account of one such unsettling encounter. The local people told him what had happened, and he scribbled:

> ... when they were boys, a beautiful white woman carrying a cross came to their lands with a cloth and a veil. She spoke to them, shouted, and harangued them in a language which they did not understand. The tribes of the Rio Colorado shot her with arrows and twice left her for dead. But, coming to life, she left by the air ... A few days later she returned many times to harangue them. . . . Since these people repeat the same story, and the places are so far apart, we surmised that perhaps the visitor was the Venerable María de Jesús de Agreda. It says in the account of her life that about the year 1630 she preached to the heathen Indians of North America and the borders of New Mexico. And sixty-eight years have passed since then, to the present year in which we are told this story by very old men, it would be possible to remember it. . . . We only note the addition that they did not understand her.

A few years ago, a scholar devoted a page of his book to refuting this story—he pointed out time-motion problems for a nun making nightly flights from seventeenth-century Spain to my desert. Frankly, I don't think his argument impressed a living soul. There is too much strangeness out there for anyone to be surprised by a flying nun.

Or a dead writer. So I'm not particularly shaken when I catch a glimpse of him now and then. Seems perfectly normal. And other people tell me they've bumped into him too.

The phone rings and I pick it up and this guy tries to explain, well, the weirdness of what he's been experiencing. The voice says, "I keep sensing he's around." And then he swiftly backtracks, pointing out he does not have a religious or mystical bent, that a lot of his friends tend toward high-risk lives and he's gotten used to burying them. But, somehow this particular death is different and he can't get a handle on why. He ends by saying softly, "I feel haunted."

I think to myself: well, it comes with the territory.

And the territory can get very strange. I am in a saloon in a fine hotel in Mesa, Arizona, talking to a visiting writer. The venue is perfect since my new acquaintance specializes in recording the destruction of the West and the hotel is a testament to this frenzy, a hulk thrown up during the savings and loan frolics of the eighties that became worthless when the house of cards collapsed, reverted to federal ownership and was peddled for a song by the munchkins who staffed our nation's most humorous agency, the Resolution Trust Corporation. He says he wants to ask me a strange question and I toss down a drink and say go right ahead. He says he's been on a kind of lecture tour and what he has noticed is that people still talk about him and shyly admit they think they've caught a glimpse of . . . well, you know.

He turns to me and asks, "Are you sure he is really dead?"

I'm lying in the sand on the plateau somewhere between God's little acre and Hole in the Rock. I've spent the morning crawling on my knees across red rock and scouting out evening primroses that have held their bloom in the shady spots. After this nature work, I've collapsed on the ground, broken open a fat volume of Mormon pioneer diaries and cracked a quart of red wine. I've also surgically removed a federal sign warning that the dirt track I'm blocking leads to danger, instant death and a fine clean drop of a couple of hundred feet into the valley below. I feel such signage is part of the unfortunate anti-Darwinian tendency of our times. Suddenly, a Volvo station wagon rumbles up and out jump four guys decked out in lycra, crash helmets, and ballet slippers with curious cleats. Moored like dead stags on the roof of the machine is a row of mountain bikes.

This gang of sprocket heads approaches me in a rush and demands to know where they are and how they can get their steeds down into the wondrous slot canyon just beyond. They wave maps at me and look grim. I point them down the dirt track now innocent of the vile sign.

They thank me, I smile and pour another hit of red wine into my Sierra cup. Here's to you, John Muir.

A few minutes after they've gone to eat their karma, I'm buried in tales of frontier fortitude, chastity, and heifer fucking when I hear a sudden roar, and then a cloud of biting sand blinds me and chokes me. I roll in a panic to the side and look down the dirt route to catch a red Cadillac convertible fishtailing toward the enormous drop. All I can hear is some idiotic cackling sound, like a hyena on mescaline.

The room is packed with people. I pull a waitress aside and she tells me this is the biggest crowd in the history of the establishment—they've never before had to wedge so many tables into the room. At the door a name tag is slapped on my chest and then suddenly hands reach out for a shake and I go from deep loneliness to instant conviviality. It is a normal human situation—you park your car in a lonely lot, walk silently toward a meeting, and then you enter a room riding a tidal wave of fellowship. Still it jolts me. The human host before me ranges from quiet good taste to adamant scruffiness, a fair survey of his readership. His widow is here, some of his friends are here, some people who became his friends after he was kind enough to die are here, and lots of people who either have no place else to go for lunch or no imagination. But the bulk of the room is these curious fans he created, strange people who seem to have little in common apart from their gluttonous appetite for his words. He created a fairly unusual readership—either people have never heard of him or have read everything he ever wrote. The B. Traven Syndrome. I fall in the latter category. One young fellow in Levi's, a cowboy shirt, and a large black Stetson explains that he has reserved one chapter of one book and will never read it so that there will always be a part of his work still to look forward to.

I briefly huddle with the other panelists, set up the speaking order, hammer out an agreement on the time limits, and do the other police work of a moderator. I know none of this will come to pass because no one who knew him is good at obeying rules or capable of maintaining order. We are a false entity: a literary panel of Luddite scum. The business meeting of the organization sponsoring the lunch lumbers along, the platters of barely warmed food are consumed. I am taken up by the good spirits of the crowd. They are all here to celebrate their own good taste, their appetite for this strange writer from a misbegotten part of the country. It is much like a meeting of penguin breeders or stamp collectors who specialize in African nations south of the Sahara. There is this contentment, a generous sigh that says, at last we are among our own kind.

The first time I met him I was not trying to meet him. I do not like writers. I'd run out of money in the early eighties and needed a job. So at about age thirty-five, I went down to the local newspaper, lied about my background, and was only hired because the big boss was absent and could not stop the abomination of my employment.

One day the city editor dispatched me to the famous man's house because he had a guest who was making waves big enough to be noted by our deadline world. So I drove out there to interview this other fellow about how he intended to save the world, what hellish techniques he was pushing on the radical environmental front, and of course to get suitably outlandish statements for an afternoon family paper. I finally found the place nestled on the bajada near some low mountains, wheeled into the drive and noted the signs warning me to turn back. I parked before a standard brick ranch-style house, the kind that clot miles of streets in my town's endless subdivisions. I saw the strange flags flying off a pole—one black, the other a rainbow vomiting a clangor of colors. As I got out of my truck an old black dog that looked half-dead made a show of being a watchful hound and then suffered a rapid energy failure.

I was approaching the door when it suddenly opened and he lumbered out, a big guy with a graying beard, quick eyes, and a small book in his hands. He said, "Would you sign this for my mother-in-law?" I looked down at this little volume and saw my first book, a thing published in the dark hours of some cursed night which then providentially fell dead from the press. I was taken aback and dutifully signed. It was the beginning of what became a friendship. The rest of that day was just business—trotting down to his writing shack by the wash, sitting out on the porch with the subject of my interview, faithfully recording his canned answers to questions he had already answered several thousand times, having a smoke, then closing my notebook (cop's off duty, guys) and indulging in free-wheeling talk. I don't remember much about it but for some reason clearly recall where I sat. His kids were very young, I think—or was it just one kid at that time?—and his wife surprised me. She was not the usual keeper-of-the-greatman but a piece of work with quick intelligent eyes, a mind of her own, direct speech, and a serious lack of awe about him and his ways.

His voice surprised me, a soft voice with the words clipped, the tone without many peaks or valleys, and sentences lucid but spiked here and there by jabs of humor and anger. It was the opposite of the typical academic voice—an instrument that does not state thoughts but pronounces them, a kind of bogus Moses voice that deadens so much of the country's talk. His voice was more sinuous, an exploring, curious rope of words that pursued, caressed, cajoled, and kicked thoughts around like empty beer cans. It was unassuming yet somehow, I thought at that moment, called attention to itself. After a spell sitting on the porch, I figured out his sly trick: he had something to say and simply said it. Voices were kind of my specialty in those days since I spent most of my time listening to them and scribbling their profundities in my notebook. I was a student of voices, mannerisms, desk tops, watch brands, clothing, physical and verbal tics, body language, come-ons, lies, deceits, blasphemies, pieties, venial sins, and false friendships. I was conditioned to the fact that people would seek to use me, play on my vanities, and cheerfully stab me in the back without notice. I loved my work and relished all the games my fellow citizens had mastered and now spun around me like a web. He performed the ultimate con on me: I couldn't figure out the con. Still can't.

I can hear the restlessness in the big room. The chairs slide and scrape a little as a general fidget sweeps through everyone. I am sitting at a kind of head table with the organization's officers, some worthies from mainline environmental outfits—one a doe-eyed woman who looks like Sylvia Plath as a backpacker ("A hike? Sorry. I've got to poke around in the oven.")

There is a stone in my guts and I cannot explain its presence. I feel disgusted that I am here to lead this discussion even though I lecture myself that I want everyone to read his books, want his widow to make a million for the kids, want the Academy, wherever the hell it lurks, to finally take notice of him. But none of this washes with me. What I really want is out of here. I want to go off to some quiet, lonely bar, have a drink, look up at televisions that blink with images but fortunately have the sound off, want to sit there and booze and say nothing and never think about what I am thinking about. Suddenly, the real problem dawns on me: I am moderating a meeting he would never attend.

It's very depressing to know and like someone and then have them die and be made into a saint. It is like watching them being buried alive. Actually, I've never been drawn to saints— as a rule they are lousy in the sack, stick-in-the-muds when it comes to music, and I'd refuse to eat in a restaurant where a saint ran the kitchen. Who wants to live in Saint Augustine's City of God?—he sure as hell never did. Nobody ever wrote on a bathroom wall, For A Good Time Call Al Schweitzer. Then I started to notice his little mannerisms becoming articles of faith or fashion. And people start asking strange questions. What did he eat? And you say testily, food. Where did he live? In a house.

I live in a time and place where to elevate someone to a pedestal means someone has the cutting knife out to geld them. And make them simple and safe and pointless, kind of like a Hallmark greeting card. This is especially irksome when the subject in question can no longer speak or snarl or offend. It entails extending the polite fraud of a eulogy into the final and ultimate statement. The only safe way to keep dead people dead is to forget they were ever alive and lived in a manner as messy and sad and happy as the rest of us. I admit we run the country by and large by doing this vicious thing to our dead presidents, but I always thought the rest of us were supposed to be exempt from such horrible punishment and allowed to sin and frolic and achieve and fail just like tomato plants and hummingbirds.

I am staring at the empty spot on the table where my lunch once sat when I am announced. I rise, stumble to the lectern, and begin braying a few words, gentle notes of scorn for the organization hosting the occasion and mild banalities about life in general, and then I introduce the first speaker. Naturally, I get the order wrong and we are off and crawling. I finally say the words I seldom say: Edward Abbey.

They come to my house on a cobblestone street late in the afternoon and press a printed invitation into my hand. I hardly hear their faint knock at first—the stereo is roaring at a steady 110 watts per channel with Neil Young's "Cowgirl in the Sand," a favorite traction song of mine. They are big guys and very brown. One takes up my offer of a beer, the other declines and has a soda pop. The soft drink devotee is not exactly a teetotaler but he has a system. From New Year's Day until Christmas Eve he never lets alcohol pass his lips. He is a religious man, a husband, a good father to a brood of children, and a hard-working manual laborer. On Christmas Eve each year he buys a bottle and stays blind, staggering drunk until New Year's Day. Generally, we have to go out on scouting expeditions to find him vomiting in some arroyo and carry him home. Then he is ready for another year of denial.

The invitation is to the wedding of the beer drinker's sister. I feel honored. I am un muy feo gringo living in a barrio in this town of six thousand souls. My days are surrounded by brown smiling faces, tropical flowers, and constant noise as the community belches, farts, sings, and laughs. I love Mexico, a vice I can neither defend nor deny. I am a junkie and here the junk is everywhere and my jones is a very light burden.

I used to go round and round with Abbey about Mexico and Mexicans. I could tell he liked it down there and found the beer cold and the people warm but always had reservations. I remember being at a kind of literary party in some old adobe in the states and another friend of mine was there who had just written a fine book on the border, probably the best such book in seventy or eighty years. Ed was standing quietly and holding a longneck beer he never drank

from, a kind of amiable statue taking in the room. Sud-
denly I noticed him locked in hard talk with my friend and
I staggered over through the throng to hear him announce,
"If you think white people in this country are going to stand
by while a bunch of Mexicans come up illegally and take
their jobs, you don't know this country." I could see that my
friend who'd just put out his border book was stunned and
trying to come up with some kind of liberal response. But his
efforts were hopeless because he had theories about illegal
immigration and Abbey had the gut responses of the nation's
mountaineer-rock-hard-white-trash hillbillies.

Later he wrote an essay, and then I reprinted part
of the essay in a magazine I was running and had people
threaten to picket my office. The passage that caused the
ruckus read:

In which case it might be wise for us as American citizens
to consider calling a halt to the mass influx of even more
millions of hungry, ignorant, unskilled, and cultural-
ly-morally-genetically impoverished people. At least until
we have brought our own affairs into order. Especially
when these uninvited millions bring with them an alien
mode of life which—let us be honest about this—is not
appealing to the majority of Americans. Why not? Because
we prefer democratic government, for one thing; because
we still hope for an open, spacious, uncrowded, and beautiful—yes, beautiful!—society, for another. The alternative,
in the squalor, cruelty, and corruption of Latin America, is
plain for all to see.

The next night I go to the wedding, which packs the
local cattleman's hall. There is a loud band, mountains of

beer, mobs of people, and outside on the street vendors are
peddling tacos, nachos, and ice cream. The whole town is
getting smashed to celebrate the marriage. The bride and
groom themselves are from large and very poor families but
this matters little. The bride's fourteen brothers and sisters
have bankrupted themselves—the wedding dress runs a
thousand or more. I am sitting at a table with my two friends
and praise the Lord! I cannot pay for a drink. The women
moving through the room are in their finest and so are the
men. The bride enters and the band breaks into a bump-and-
grind worthy of a striptease palace, and she seems to handle
the beat well and wears a vast smile on her face.

My eyes roam and feed, my ear sucks in the sounds,
my mind churns and my tongue is stilled. I am in that zone
of fraud and apology, the industrial world wallowing in the
ceremonies of the non-industrial world. And usually in such
instances, I, along with almost everyone else, choose silence
rather than truth. Outside the walls, far out there where the
music falls away, the night hugs the dying land. I am living
in a forest that is disappearing and there are explanations
of agribusiness, hunger, development, ignorance, greed,
lack of planning, and environmental unawareness. These
words tinkle like little bells but can never form a true chord
or fuse themselves into actual music. Out there in the vast
dying, the forest is disappearing, the babies are being born
and then dying from diarrhea, the drug trade is butcher-
ing men, women, and children, the food is scant, the hips
lean, the teeth bad, the eyes tired, the cattle mere bones, the
ground screaming from pain, the birds vanishing and their
songs trailing off to silence—all because of human numbers.
Everything else is a detail and everyone with a brain and
a healthy set of loins knows it. The beer, the conspicuous

consumption of the evening, the good spirits of my friends
buying endless rounds they cannot really afford, the smile of
the bride's father—my mentor—as he shyly shuffles past in
bedroom slippers and new jeans, all these touches of won-
derment and pleasure intoxicate me. I could go on forever
writing rhythms to the beat of the night, the joy I feel in
being accepted by these people as a friend.

Ed would like it here tonight, I know that. In fact,
he would use up my space and soon be hitting on one of the
eager women, his eyes gleaming to the lust and laughter of
the group. He would stay for hours and never lean over and
make one serious comment, or natter about the sociologi-
cal implications, or denounce the culture of the celebrants.
And they would like him, see him as a macho, and as very
friendly, as someone who did not check out the color of their
skin before he considered the heart and soul in their eyes. All
the babies on the breast at this festivity would win a smile
from his bearded face. And the various campesinos would
laugh and call him barbón, and he'd tug at his beard and
laugh and say he was muy viejo, and they would hand him
a beer and he'd pretend to drink and they'd notice but say
nothing and never mock him because they believe in polite-
ness and stupidity and beautiful women and dancing and
stars in the sky and the seconds and minutes and hours of
this night they have all sacrificed so much to create.

Of course, Abbey isn't here, he's dead as a doornail
and now cannon fodder for obituaries, summings-up, and
various literary winding sheets. The New York Times,
after pissing on his head for decades, has entombed him
securely in a two-page eulogy. Well, I'm not Ed—where
the hell did he disappear to?—and I suck down the beers
greedily, deposit my present for the bride on the heaped

table, wink at her father when she walks past and make suitably lustful sounds which I can see bring pleasure to his face. I can remember sitting up one night with the old man in a big building where he was the night watchman. I was drinking and the seventy-five-year-old goat was talking dirty, as was his custom. Suddenly he noticed a dark and furry ball of daddy longleg spiders on the wall, scuttled over on his old legs and said, "Panocha," slang for pussy, and then proceeded to move his hips as if he were fucking the ball of spiders, and I laughed loudly and he smiled at me in gratitude. And I wrote a book to save the forest that was collapsing hourly around the town and never mentioned the constant killings, the countless fields of opium poppies and marijuana in the forest, the fact that part of the funding for this wonderful wedding Ed and I were attending came from the drug business. My forest book does not have a fifteen-year-old girl cut in half by an Uzi but my forest does. And Ed wrote polemics about brown hordes eating the earth, dying planets, undemocratic cultures and human tides.

So I don't have an Abbey problem, I've just got an Abbey friend who is and was a bundle of contradictions. As am I. Hate the sin, love the sinner, a saying as old as sin and sinners. The only thing that has changed is that virtue remains a relative constant, but sin can now disguise itself as virtue in this global death dance of eating our own bodies and killing our earth.

Is Abbey childish? racist? sexist? cynical? a fake? a fraud? a hypocrite? (This is my favorite charge.)

Does your mommy wear army boots?

Colors now, colors chasing the music. My eyes don't focus so good but I'm seeing more by the beer as I let go of the numbers, the theories, the charts, the stench of death and smell the scent of a woman walking by in a blazing blue dress with a baby in her arms. I am happy for the whole fucking human race at this instant, even the parts I know are wrong, and the parts lifting my spirits as this wedding glides effortlessly through the tropical night. Somewhere on the mountain a boa constrictor hunts just as I prowl in this room full of sweating humanity.

Hours later I stagger out into the narrow streets of the old town. It is somewhere between midnight and dawn and I am somewhere between half-drunk and drunk. I'm walking down the bumpy lane and the air is still warm and heavy with the scent of flowers. I piss against the wall of a house when suddenly headlights nail me and this obnoxious horn starts bleating. I look up and this car roars past. All I can see is the flash of a red convertible, the outline of some old goat at the wheel, and as the machine disappears the delighted face of a twenty-year-old Mexican girl sitting next to the driver as she turns her head and stares at me with a smile. The fucking driver flips a Tecate can over his shoulder and high into the air out the back and hits me smack dab in the middle of my forehead.

The program unfolds for an hour and a half or two hours. I really don't know, it seems like forever. In between speakers I bounce up like a jack-in-the-box and do a little patter. The room stays reverently silent most of the time and seizes upon each quip or joke with relief. I half listen. Everyone is doing a good job—catching the audience's attention, giving that telling detail to jump-start an anecdote, avoiding a dry reading of a speech. Still, my lids grow heavy and my mind drifts. I am poor at remembering the past and much better at inhabiting it. Things that *were* actually exist to me. I am the enemy of history and yet a card-carrying member of the dead.

We meet in a Mexican restaurant near my office. I am working sixty, seventy, eighty hours a week putting out my magazine and he rags me about this venture. I'm not quite sure why, because I never really asked what his reason or reasons were. For me the magazine is an obsession and I am at my happiest when I am obsessed. We launched the thing in a house on skid row and now it is mildly prospering and the investors, in a seizure of pomposity, have moved us to fancy offices along the Rillito, a small desert stream that my town has systematically murdered. I am living a careless life of random fornication, alcohol, work and black coffee. Sometimes I sleep on my office floor. My backpack is buried in some closet encased with spider webs. I no longer think about wandering the desert again— I'm grateful for just a few idle moments in the daylight. I've gone maybe two years at this point without a day off, a seven-day-a-week treadmill. Still, we meet from time to time, a kind of pit stop for me in the endless race to put the magazine solidly into the promised land of black ink. Usually, he calls, and I think, what the hell, the way I'm living is screwy—not a term he would use, much too mild for him—and I say sure.

I always get there first, I'm a fiend for meaningless punctu-
ality. The restaurant has finished its noon rush but still is noisy
because of its ocean of hard red tiles. I order a bowl of menudo
and wait, making notes in my new workaholic manner about
business to attend to that afternoon at the magazine. I run with
rich and sick boys now, I'm a member of the Chamber of Commerce. I drink with advertisers and give an ear to the town's
scumbag movers and shakers. It's part of the racket. It's also
part of me—how can you play if you don't play to win?

I feel someone standing in front of my table and look up
and it's Abbey in his clean, pressed Levi's, old shirt with neatly
stitched patches, vest, and raggedly groomed beard. He is rustling a few sheets of paper as he sits down and has that telltale
gleam in his eye that always indicates he is in his Tom Sawyer
mode. Here I am a respectable magazine editor and part owner
to boot and now I have to deal with an irresponsible American
teenager. I feel like lashing out with some bit of wisdom such
as, "The business of America is business." Or perhaps, knowing his vices, "What this country needs is a good five-cent
cigar." But I hold myself in check and affect an air of endless
patience with this callow youth.

He is restless. I can tell that the Delight Maker is stirring
beneath his laconic speech and low soft voice. He has a plan,
he announces.

"I am going to run for mayor," he lets on. "Of course I'm
not going to run a real campaign with all those speeches and
debates. I'm just going to announce, issue this statement"—
and here he rustles his little sheaf of papers like a gourd rattle
in a medicine dance—"and then disappear with Clarke and the
kids and have a relaxing month or two."

Ah, *vox populi* is smiling right across from my bowl of tripe and hominy. I can hear the boom, boom, boom of Walt Whit-man, the chanting of Vachel Lindsay, and Carl Sandburg is tuning up his instrument to give me ditties on the importance of rutabagas to the national soul. Edward Abbey, child of classical anarchism, heir to Ethan Allen and the Green Moun-tain Boys, illegitimate son of Daniel Shays, has come to claim his patrimony. "Anarchism is democracy taken seriously," the noted political savant and adviser of presidents, Edward Abbey, has scribbled. He has a childlike faith in the voodoo of the early republic, a belief that the best possible world is one where power is dispersed. He is born to hate limousines, steady work, and the factory whistle. He is the stone-crazy Jeffersonian anxious to follow the great man's injunction to water that tree of liberty with blood each and every generation. He is a religious fanatic about anarchism, small "d" democ-racy, and individual rig dry, folks. All of his books rest on this foundation of dull, philosophical arguments about anarchism and he has dined on endless and obscure nineteenth-century texts written by deviant Russians or angry toilers. And now, I, a card-carrying member of the Chamber of Commerce, must confront this naïf youngster. Unfortunately, I am not prop-erly armed for this task since I hate all forms of authority, am against all governments, and, truth be known, am not keen on the current mayor—a half-witted creature whom I steadily lampoon in my magazine (though, to be honest, I worry that my criticisms of this political tyro may be seen as child abuse). As a legit businessman, I am, to use Winston Churchill's won-derfully venomous phrase, a sheep in sheep's clothing.

Ed is leaning forward now, thundering his announcement of his willingness to throw his battered and befouled hat into the ring. I can sense he envisions large drunken rallies at the finale of his campaign, with kegs of beer nestled in mountains of ice, smoke rising off the cook fires where whole oxen slowly rotate on spits. No doubt there will be Abbey Girls, fierce river-running women who do elaborately choreographed routines with oars and then challenge any foolish males in the audience to arm wrestle them for serious money. He'll pick some movement from the din of Charles Ives' works for his theme song and be backed by an itinerant group of classically trained mariachis who will be fueled by mescal and *mota*. My entire community will be laid waste by vandals purporting to be precinct workers and his party's symbol on the ballot will be a large monkey wrench on a field of black. And he'll be hectoring me constantly for play in my magazine, demanding space to address the key issues facing the electorate, things like the war on the economy (how do we stop this industrial beast from growing and spewing out more and more of that evil money?) and how to kill growth, and timely suggestions on easy steps to return my town to the Pleistocene.

Fortunately for my new station in life, I see a flaw in this wicked plan and a way out for sound burghers such as myself.

"Ed," I intone thoughtfully, "you don't live in the city."

His brow furrows and darkens.

"You mean you've got to live in this hellhole to run for mayor?" He is crestfallen. It's clear, he never anticipated such a chickenshit requirement . . .

My fingers softly rub the fabric of the tablecloth as the program rumbles on. I drink ice-cold water and wait it out. One friend is explaining a trip into the desert with Abbey and then somehow seizes a magic carpet and takes off for parts unknown where he castigates whatever meets his spleen. Everyone is trying to do the right thing. This is dangerous ground, but Abbey's friend is negotiating the terrain with the right tone of irreverence. Desert worship is a suspicious matter to desert rats. It is as if talking about what is out there will diminish what is out there. Also, as a group, we feel damn foolish admitting what we feel out there. The lightest utterance is liable to launch a stampede of mush-headed-crystal-gazing-safe-sex-tofu-munching souls into our playground, where they will set up prayer wheels and disturb the scorpions, tarantulas, Gila monsters, rattlesnakes and kissing bugs. So we lie about where we have been and deny what we have felt. And even when we get together and the blinds are pulled, the door bolted, the trip wires set on the perimeter and the armed sentries posted with laser-sighted, fully automatic weapons, we still are loathe to utter the words. I can't recall ever talking to Ed about what the desert means or is or does. Not a word. Not safe, you know. Besides there is really not much to say. Some things just are and you thank God for that and keep your lips sealed.

Abbey made a semi-career out of writing about the desert by skirting the very essence of what he was writing about:

Marching on, north, I follow this condemned jeep road as it meanders toward the mountains. Why do I *do* this sort of thing? I don't know. I've been doing this sort of thing for thirty-five years and still don't know why. Don't even care why. It's not logical—it's pathological. We go on and on, our whole lives, never changing, repeating ourselves with minor variations. We do not change. Bruckner spent his life writing the same symphony nine times, trying to get it just right. Seeking perfection, Mozart wrote his single symphony forty-eight times. We cannot change. Saul on the road to Damascus, struck by the lightning of revelation, turns his coat inside out, drops the S and adds the P, and goes right on.

Right on fantasizing. And here I walk on the old devil's road.
. . . Under a clear sky. Marching. Singing. Marching. . . .

Delirium. Walking along, I realize I've forgotten to but-
ton my fly. My prick is hanging out, dangling like a banner
in defeat. Like the nose of a possum. Like the pseudopod of
an uncircumcised amoeba. . . . But what the hell—it looks
so nice out today I think I'll leave it out all afternoon . . .

He used to lecture me about disguising place names, telling
nobody nothing and such like. Still I always argued with him,
claiming it was too late, there were too many people loose on
the land for secrecy to save anything and that we had to label
places, build partisans, coalitions, all manner of dreary orga-
nizations if we were going to save anything at all. Basically, a
boring and pointless argument since we both had good answers
that would never work in this exploding planet.

Of course, he was responding to a deep hurt from an unfortunate section of *Desert Solitaire* that launched thousands of
maniacs into the empty ground and pulverized one of his
favorite backwaters of the Colorado Plateau. In many ways,
the whole damn book seems to me a curse. I dismiss out-of-
hand his typical fraud about having scribbled it on the bar top
of a whorehouse in Nevada, but the book did two things: it
made his reputation and dwarfed everything else he thought
he did. When it came out, I read it and thought, ah, it's okay.
I have a hard time getting excited about books I agree with
and seem fated to fixate on words that prod me or threaten
my world. Abbey stated that the land and wilderness have a
value in and of themselves and fuck the industrial tourists and
the corporate hyenas, that national parks should outlaw automobiles and dismiss their search and rescue squads so that my
fellow citizens could find a good death or at least put a little

sizzle back into their lives, and finally he refused to find God in the land but merely something bigger than words can label. By writing all this he said the obvious and so I thought, so what? I was wrong. For hundreds of thousands of decent people it was either a revelation or at the very least their flesh made word. The book raised a strange ill-organized army of lovers of what is beyond our control, the wild and free ground. It's one of the few books I've ever reread, kind of like sniffing the old cork of a memorable bottle of wine.

But getting back to the curse, it is very simple. Edward Abbey did not want to be seen as a nature writer for good and noble reasons: the genre demands unseemly vows more restrictive than joining the Benedictine order. Nor did he want to be seen as an essayist. He kept mumbling to me from time to time that he had finished with this nature writing, desert writing stuff. For him there was only one holy grail: The Novel. This disorder can be explained. He was a man of his time. For his generation, coming out of World War II, the Great American Novel was the white buffalo of the sacred medicine. Nonfiction was just a gig to make money but the novel was the true proof of worth and the only serious method of plumbing the depths of the nation, the planet, and the human soul. Edward Abbey the desert rat squandered some years at cheap wine parties in the apartments of New York with the other young tyros seeking lit crit's heavyweight title. And then when he came to ground in the American West, he saw the rise of other callow youths from those days in New York—the Updikes, the Mailers—and he thought shit, I can take those guys out and I will.

I'm from a later generation, one that has seen American fiction denatured and neutered by creative writing departments and can hardly take the novel seriously as a form—except for the exorcising of adulterous demons among infrequently sexually active academic scribblers. In the 1920s, Theodore Dreiser took clips from a fine murder and refashioned them into a huge novel called *An American Tragedy*. In the 1960s, Truman Capote, an established fiction writer, took some clips from a tasty Kansas slaughter and refashioned them into a nonfiction book called *In Cold Blood*. The flight from the novel was echoed in other genres as the American university grew fat on its incestuous relationship with what Dwight David Eisenhower warned in his farewell address was a growing and dangerous military-industrial complex. The art of serious biography fled the deadly hands of historians and found safe haven in the care of laypeople who were interested in past lives. Poetry disappeared into the Academy to become a dead language like Latin or classical Greek.

None of these changes seemed to dent Abbey's skull and he remained a faithful lover of the dream girl of his youth— The Novel. He launched a kind of one-man hunt for the last woolly mammoth: something he called the Fat Masterpiece. And by this weird standard he judged himself and his work. So the novels, the whole bunch of them, were to him his real stuff, and the rest, the polemical volumes of essays periodically issued like terrorist weapons into the republic, the curious and wrathy meditations like *Desert Solitaire*, were, well, something else and in the end something less than The Novel.

Naturally, I never agreed with him, but I'm hardly the person to quarrel with somebody else's passion, particularly if the somebody else is a friend and an obsessive type—I'm a sucker for obsessive people. Life is too short not to be a maniac. And then, when he finally rolled his Fat Masterpiece out the door, cunningly disguised with the title *The Fool's Progress: An Honest Novel*, he was greeted with something like horror because his novel bristled with racial jokes and sexual jokes and was powered by a hero who was not very heroic but seemed to be a well-read example of American white trash, a chap with a resemblance to one Edward Abbey. I remember reading the *New York Times* review, which quietly smothered the book with condescension and mild contempt. Other reviews were more vitriolic in their distaste. Well, that's life, but when you've run out your string and you know you're dying, it's not a wonderful way to see your Fat Masterpiece received. Still, with the single exception of one review, he never said anything to me about the matter. He'd been flogged for years by his foes and slowly murdered with praise by his devotees. I think he'd gotten fairly used to being a thing, this fraud he'd foisted on the world called Edward Abbey, and he simply moved on to his next book, his last as it happened, and naturally it was a novel.

I liked the Fat Masterpiece, and, loyal friend that I was, reviewed it in my magazine. Of course, I referred to the title as *A Fool's Errand*, a slip that Abbey pointed out to me in his timely way. But I also loved his polemics, a fact he accepted with churlish good humor. And what I liked about the polemics was not just their ferocity and glee but their moral grounding. I don't know how to look at the world except morally, regardless of my sinful ways. I hate the clever and prefer love mixed with dollops of indignation. And so did he, though I'm not sure he'd want to admit to such a thing. And I like to laugh. Things are too serious for me to take them seriously . . .

Christ, the next speaker has somehow made the pilgrimage to the lectern. Somewhere in my wanderings through memory, I must have leapt up, said the appropriate words of introduction, and made it back to my perch. Apparently, I'm flying on automatic pilot. Ummmm, I peer out at the room and all the faces now have the look of the church lady. I notice for the first time that they are all white and feel vague discomfort at this fact. I am biased against blondes. A woman once told me it was because blondes lack brain juice. Brunettes, she explained, had brain juice—that's what puts the color into the fur on their skulls. Could be. More field research is called for, endless studies with rigorous inkblot tests, math quizzes, three-dimensional puzzles, and hapless subjects parachuted into the wilderness armed with nothing more than fishhooks, the old Testament, and dental floss.

I remember sitting in my office, a stuffed trout hanging from the ceiling, piles of unreadable manuscripts composting quietly on the floor, and I rip open an envelope and a letter spills out from Fort Llatikcuf. Some imbecilic reader is harping about the advertisements in my periodical, calling my attention to the fact that after a diligent examination and tally, it is clear to him that the last issue's ads had nineteen brunettes—and not all of them, the reader notes, reeking of pulchritude—and only three blondes, although an allowance is made for the fact that they are creatures both nubile and well worth having. Then there is this curious parenthetical caveat, "(not for publication, the wife you know.)" I scan down to the signature and find, in the moronic hand so typical of the semiliterate, "Edward Abbey, His Mark."

Ah, the purity issue. The redneck sitting there while classical music purred in his writing shack and sucking on a big ugly cigar. The culinary expert stressing the importance of fried eggs and ample portions of pig meat. The guy who couldn't have a drink for years, claiming he roared down the nation's highways pitching beer cans out the windows so our descendants could easily discover densely packed and linear mineral belts. Mr. Save-The-Wilderness lovingly recording his various journeys with machines into the wild country, trips which it seemed inevitably ended with the total destruction of his vehicle. Mr. Anarchist—Power to the People!—studding his works with racial jokes. I am particularly keen on his repertoire of Oriental jests since my son is half-Japanese by heritage. I remember sitting there half the night surgically removing this shit from a chunk of *The Fool's Progress* he gave me for publication in the magazine. I mentioned this hobby of his after this particular bout of text cleansing, and he smiled kind of shyly like it was his job to say it and my job to stop him. Hell, I don't know. I do remember haggling with him over the price for the excerpt. He insisted on nothing, and I said that something for nothing is nothing. I won and gave him my usual rate, a pittance.

But I understood the deep spring this was flowing from, the source of this need to offend. No, it wasn't simply the cracker in him boiling up and out. Nor was it some pathological need to appear cantankerous, though both these forces festered in him and erupted from time to time. It was freedom.

It was the archaic and vital personal need to answer to no one, to kowtow to no one, to refuse to be shelved and labeled by anyone. It was, my friends, the dread of the fucking rules. This river runs deep and usually silent in my nation, but it runs nonetheless. It is the enemy of decorum, solutions, and safe streets and it always scares the horses and upsets the women and children. It is the hurricane, the flood, the tornado, the earthquake, the forest fire, the drought, the blizzard, the late August freeze, the spread of Bang's in the herd, the plague of locusts, the actual plague itself, the barroom brawl, the V-8 roaring at 110, the hatred of seat belts, motorcycle helmets, the dread of airbags, the acting up in Sunday school, the love of sloth, the attraction to and scorn for white picket fences, the love of guns and outrage over unnecessary noise. It is the American before the American government arrived to post the letters and give you a number. And it is a pain in the ass, at least to me, since I share its vices.

I own a bunch of guns, disgusting things like Colt .45s, a .9mm with two big clips, .357 Magnums, and the like. I hate the sound of guns. For most of the past year I was the lord and servant of a ranch with no neighbors and I would not let a gun be fired on the place—scared the birds, I'd tell my infrequent visitors, and I meant it. But I keep them all loaded and close at hand because of them, whoever the hell THEM is, and because I cannot put my faith in order and decorum no matter how much I crave such things. I know it is a messy world right down to the wild salvias growing by the door and I do not intend to be lulled into the illusion of sanctuary and utopia.

I don't think he did either. It's not in the blood and it sure as hell is not in the history. All the quiet moments are cherished interludes between the storms of an increasingly louder Wagnerian opera. In long and short, a contradiction.

There is no peaceful garden, in fact in the long run there is no garden. Yes, I know that Cain slew Abel but look what happened. It's a flow, a biting, yipping, rising and falling flow and the best you can hope for is to be kind and loving and wary. A cold beer now and then doesn't hurt, and be sure to pay attention to music, life may not exist without song. I put out a good hundred pounds of birdseed every month, I'm hot for the song.

So we're all left facing this disgusting mirror of ourselves, this creature whom one reviewer of *A Fool's Progress* thumbnailed:

From a distance, Abbey may sound like an environmental-
ist, but only from a distance. Environmentalists generally
pay at least lip service to the rights and values of Native
Americans. Abbey lumps Indians with other "minorities"—
women, Hispanics, Jews, well-to-do WASPS—as enemies
of both the land and its rightful inheritors: Appalachian
hillbilly white trash. . . . *The Fool's Progress* shows that the
nativist hostility is as much a part of Edward Abbey as is his
love of the Western landscape and sky.

Or consider the profile published in a skin magazine in the
early eighties by Morton Kamins:

We . . . continue our philosophical causerie; more of
Abbey's "crank, crackpot views." He is in favor of low
productivity, a contracting economy, tax policies to actively
encourage negative population growth. A population of
fifty million would make the United States livable again . . .
    I suggest that part of his problem may be his literary
politics which are irrefutably atrocious . . .

The cunning critic nailing Abbey for his crackpot views and
stupid, petulant, literary quarrels is . . . well, Edward Abbey.
He wrote the profile, faked the author's name and address,
tried to peddle it to *Esquire*, and when that failed, got it printed
in *Gallery*, a third- or fourth-rate soft-porn rag. This kind of
nonsense was a recurrent thing. A friend of his was over at his
house once for breakfast when Abbey realized two reporters
were coming to interview him. He tried to talk his friend into
pretending to be him and faking the interview.
    What is to be done with this unseemly creature? He appears
housebroken but just look at this mess on the rug. Why won't

Spot behave? Jesus, look now, he's jumped the fence and is gone for the night. Gonna be chasing deer or cattle, watch the hen house. Maybe he'll tangle with another skunk. Why can't he learn?

I think part of the problem lies in the way he wrote. People could actually understand what he was saying and this quickly pissed them off. He wrote direct sentences with active verbs and the music displayed a deep suspicion of adjectives, except for comic effect. He sounded so offhanded that the reader thought he'd just dashed it off. In fact he sounded a lot like the guy who is sitting next to you on the barstool talking over a beer. The reality of the sentences is the opposite of the effect. He wrote very tightly and it is difficult to cut a line or a word. Naturally, it took a lot of work to make it all look so easy. His drafts had marks all over them and lines writhing like snakes indicating where a phrase or sentence should be moved. All this effort results in an almost laconic voice punctuated from time to time by bombast, invective, and high jinks. I remember once, when I worked at the newspaper, I arranged a kind of op-ed piece face-off on growth between Abbey and a local car dealer. Everything was going fine until the dealer discovered who his adversary would be. He immediately canceled. I was not surprised. The dealer would have submitted some piece of mush cranked out by a public relations flack and would have faced live ammo from a cracker Gatling gun. So Ed consistently fucked up in our deconstructionist age. His meaning was unmistakable, a serious fault. And he seemed to be enjoying himself, too. A lot of people can't tolerate such things . . .

Who's up now? I've done it again, sleepwalked through another introduction. This has got to stop, for God's sake, I'm the moderator. Abbey's widow, Clarke, is sitting at a table up front and God only knows what all this affectionate malarkey means to her.

I remember that day I met her, Abbey mumbling about asking me to autograph that book for his mother-in-law and then this fresh-faced woman appearing, about thirty years his junior, and she is moving with a quiet air of certainty. I go in the house and there is a sloppy bookcase with too much tonnage for decent order and on a wall various pencil marks where some child's growth is being recorded. The eyes catch my attention, focused and looking into me. I think, I wonder if this will last. None of the others have. And it did, though God knows how. Somehow Ed couldn't quite figure out how to break her or drive her nuts. But I'm certain he tried . . .

I never once met him for lunch or at any other occasion in a public place where his eyes didn't wander after fifteen or twenty seconds to track a woman walking past. I can't speak for others, but I know a roving boy with a weather eye peeled.

Once, when I was working at the newspaper, I got a call at home from a reporter who'd stumbled onto the fact that Edward Abbey, the enemy of growth, had applied under someone else's name to have his piddling acres on the edge of the sprawl rezoned for higher density. As I listened to the woman's excited voice, I knew what was going on: that a huge subdivision was going to surround his hideaway and he had a choice of moving out now and letting the buyer rezone it to cash in or rezoning it and taking some money with him. The whole situation had a wonderful quality to it since the person wheeling and dealing downtown for the soon-to-descend subdivision was a former mayoral candidate who'd run his campaigns under the aegis of Cactus Power. God, I love my town.

Anyway, she'd called because she knew he was my friend

and how in the hell should she proceed in this delicate matter. I gave her his home phone, I said call him and tell him you're coming out. And then print it. Rules of the game, no favors for friends. Pay your money and you get, we pray, an honest newspaper. So she went out and talked to Ed and Clarke—"We thought she was understanding and our friend," Clarke told me later—and then filed it. And, not surprisingly given Ed's flaming reputation as the enemy of developers in town, he came out looking like a desert warrior who was a hypocrite because he took the fast buck when it came his way. This was not true, but the newspaper comes out every twenty-four hours and there are some messes along the way. Later when I told Ed and Clarke I'd essentially orchestrated the coverage, neither one of them seemed to believe it—the business is an iron cross. For years afterward when people learned Ed Abbey was my friend, they would bring up that story to discredit his unseemly ways. I was not surprised. We all need to discredit anyone who threatens us—it is a lot easier than considering their ideas. Anyway, that is not the point of this anecdote.

The next day when the story hit print, Ed called up the reporter—a blonde woman in her early twenties, as it happened—and said let's have breakfast. She said okay. He said he was going to Phoenix and did she want to go along?

Or one of my ex-wives was at a dance recital sitting with her friend's mother while her friend performed. Ed was there. During intermission, my wife's friend came out into the audience to see her mother and Ed sauntered over and said are you doing anything later?

Or the woman who worked in the bookstore who told me she was disappointed because Ed never hit on her.

Or Ed leaning across a table while we had a cup of coffee and advising me on a fine technique for book tours and signings. When a pretty woman comes up to get a book signed, he counseled me, be sure to write your motel and room number in it. You'll be surprised, he continued, how often it works.

Or . . . what's the point?

As Ed wrote in his journal about twelve years before he died,

> But we'll struggle on through and outlive our tears,
> Whether marriage be a joy or a joke;
> I don't give a damn if it takes forty years,
> I'm cleaving to Clarke till I croak.

And he did. Still, he'd write stuff in his books like, how was he supposed to singlehandedly repeal two million years of simian biology? Now it seems we are all supposed to have an opinion about his behavior and I figure we ought to all go ahead and have an opinion. But the only reason we can have an opinion is because of the record he left in print and in public. I kind of prefer what he got out of it—a life.

People like to comment on Abbey's attitudes toward women. On the one hand, he tended to defend himself by stating he had a daughter and wife and wanted the same rights for them as for himself, and I don't doubt he meant it. On the other hand, many of his readers noticed he paid a lot of attention to how women looked in his writings and seemed to see them as sex objects. In short, was he sexist? Hell, I suppose so. It's not an unusual condition, in fact those free of this awful malady seem to be the great rarities. Was he the dreaded philanderer? Well, I don't have videotapes on the matter but I don't doubt he was. Did he have female writer friends and help them get published? Sure, what's so odd about that? Did he always keep one eye peeled for a pretty woman? He always did when I was around him. I must say he carried his affliction with some grace and labored mightily under this burden. I think everyone would save themselves a lot of time and trouble if they just concluded he was guilty of every vice and ism known to man—except for writing badly or putting lies on paper. You'll never be able to clean him up. So wear nice white gloves if you are forced by cruel circumstances to dip into his works.

I was driving my truck one day when a friend of mine looked at all the cutouts of naked women I'd plastered all over the cab and mud flaps. She remarked how much she hated my idea of ornaments. Fair enough. I'd equipped my machine with this host of naked ladies after living a year in Mexico and then being forced to make a dead-tick landing back in the States. (I am now an Arrested Sex Addict and have stripped off most of the doodads save the mud flaps.) What I noticed immediately upon my reentry to the States was that the people in the checkout lines looked sad, that the men and women walked as if they were suffering serious hormone deprivation and that everyone in the land of plenty looked and acted angry. I revolted and festooned my truck with images of the flesh in much the same way as a Transylvanian never leaves home without garlic and a crucifix. When I would return to my place in Mexico from time to time, not one—not one single soul—ever commented on my rolling skin magazine. And I know why. They take such matters in stride. I lived next door to the town's leading *jato*, homosexual, who wore capri pants, pumps, and lots of makeup. The neighborhood ladies would regularly descend on him for permanents, haircuts, and fifteen-round styling bouts. He sold me beer at the local *cerveceria* and I never heard anyone remark on his striking garb or predilections. In the land of macho, there was an acceptance of the obvious—human diversity.

Back in the States, statements—both spoken and written—were scrutinized to see if they were appropriate. And worse than that, nobody looked happy or at ease with their bodies or their lives. I have seldom seen a woman in Mexico who did not move as if she knew all men desired her or watched a man walk through a market who did not think of himself as God's personal gift to women. I never heard an adult yell at a child, or shout at another adult except to hail them. I never saw anybody run as if late to an appointment. I'm sure it happens, but not in the regular course of business. I often think of Mexico—a country Abbey both dreaded and found attractive—when I listen to people flail around about his work. In a nation of sex-obsessed saints and greedy selfish liberals, in a nation approaching a racial chasm grounded on growing poverty and a rampant lack of compassion, there seems to be a deep need to determine if someone else's thoughts are proper rather than well stated, or true, or funny, or felt. Edward Abbey was not cut out for such a world.

He will never be what you approve of, though he will (with alarming frequency) be what you secretly think but are afraid to say or admit to. And he will most often act out the one thing you dream of but cannot do: live your life regardless of the opinions of others. He will write novels where women are cagey and nimble sexual objects, where other races are the butt of jokes, where the appetite for violence is admitted and at times relished, and where his own stupidity is deliciously recorded and mocked. He will be incapable of running more than, say, a hundred pages without appalling you. And worse yet, he won't seem to care all that much. And even worse than that, you'll find yourself laughing along with him and hope no one is listening in. Things bawdy will not make him blush, things hard will not make him cringe, but things dishonest will make him yell. When he is done with you your head will be full of ideas and you'll agree with some and disagree with others. But you won't forget, that'll be the hell of it, the memory will not mercifully fade. Especially about the ground around you. I'm sorry, but the bastard will have stolen your eyes and left you with his. But don't fret. If sometimes it seemed like his head was full of shit, still, he always could see pretty clearly.

In a nation of overweight people who are inwardly starving, he never seemed to hide his appetites. The demented desire for greasy food, soft breasts, blond hair, big machines, loud guns, good books, classical music, and sleazy saloons was part of the package. Look, it's a matter of taste, not theology. And frankly, I don't want Ed cooking in my kitchen—I like all that Oriental chow he made fun of. But that's not how a sane person judges a book or an idea. If they did, Neitzsche wouldn't be in print. Nor would Saint Francis of Assisi and his *Little Flowers*. As my dad told me when I was but a boy, "If everyone were the same, everyone would want my squaw."

It is years ago, there is a knock on the door at night. I open it and a woman is standing there. She says, "Where were you last week? I had to fuck a perfect stranger." She wheels on her heels and stalks off. Am I supposed to judge her or record her or approve of her? Or simply try to understand her? I am sitting in a yard and a friend says, "I can't stand it when I see a white woman with a black guy." I am listening to an ex-convict laugh. He has killed at least eleven men in the joint and God knows how many on the outside. His torso is blue black from jailhouse tattoos. I am reading a book and the damn fool author is touting how to blow up Glen Canyon Dam. I am listening to the radio and discover my nation's army is plunging into yet another nation without an invitation. I have an opinion on just about everything—except the propriety of other people having ideas and opinions.

But I realize this talk is of little consequence. It's hardly a First Amendment issue, or even a good taste question. It is about a failure of nerve. I live in a time of fear and anger and it expresses itself by the dread of expression itself. Well, as one headline over an obituary essay about Ed put it: "Born a hundred years too late, died a hundred years too soon." Hope not, I haven't got a century left in me. It's a strange era. One when we cannot seem to face differences. Ah, the reviews say he couldn't create real women. I never have read a review that said a female novelist couldn't create real men. I live in a time when a woman can and does say you will never understand because you are a man. But men are rash if they say, you will never understand because you are a woman. Well, you take the time God gives you and belly up to the bar of life, order your favorite and dream on and on and on. There is always morning and fresh hopes.

You just don't get it, do you?

It's a year or so after his death—I'm not so good at dates—and we're all sitting in my rundown house looking at a screen. Back in 1986, Ed took a trip back to his native ground in Home, Pennsylvania, and a friend of mine went along with him for the ride. He remembers Ed being sick quite a bit then with the illness that finally claimed him and getting medicine on the road from various postal drops—drugs his wife wasn't mailing but some other woman was. The slides flashing up on the screen are the skeleton of *A Fool's Progress* and in some cases literally document scenes from the novel. I watch and remember kidding Ed, after meeting one of the people he used for a character in *The Monkey Wrench Gang*, that he didn't seem to have much of an imagination.

My friend is managing the slide show and Clarke and I are sitting on the couch as the pictures flash past. There is one vignette in the novel of the main character crossing a river in the Midwest with his truck and dog on a small ferry. In the book, a good-looking woman runs the ferry. Suddenly, there's Ed up on the screen in the middle of a small river with his arms wrapped around a good-looking woman and he's got this big shit-eating grin. At the same time I say, "That's my boy" and Clarke says, "That son-of-a-bitch." And then we laugh. . . .

Anarchism, that's the word I hear now as I tune back into the program. I can see people I know out there in the sea of faces, the publisher who gave me a job on a newspaper when I was dead broke, had no real credentials, and lied about the ones I claimed. That was back in my visit to the land of objectivity and empathy, a world Abbey knew by reputation more than by experience. Newspapers were not his thing. Every once in a while he would drop in at the magazine and toy with the idea of writing a real story, say, cover a murder trial. He wanted to see if he could simply report what he witnessed, empathize with and explain people on both sides of the issue. He never got around to it because dropping dead got in the way. It would have been an interesting experiment since he gave little evidence in his work of such aptitudes. He was an advocate and critic and his novels are peopled with walking ideas and dominated by projections of his own personality and beliefs. Fortunately, for a lot of us, visiting inside Edward Abbey's head was an interesting tour of duty.

He'd get a little disturbed at my willingness to disappear into the lives and minds of others—wheeler-dealer developers, contract killers, drug dealers, savings and loan boys.

Sometimes there would be a note functioning as a humorous reprimand and a kind of silent question that ran, how could you? Well, everybody has their differences. Somehow I did not have a problem sympathetically describing acts and attitudes and ideas I despised—in fact, while I was describing such things it never consciously crossed my mind what I thought about them. (Christ, when I was a reporter condemned to covering sex crimes, I attended rape therapy in the joint and outpatient sexual child abuse therapy in my crazed desire to understand the people who did such things.) I remember after doing one such long piece on Charles Keating, the national symbol of greed and theft in the eighties, I received a note from Abbey on the piece saying that my hard labors had achieved the quintessence of rottenness. Well, at least I excelled.

As I listen to his friends rumble on about what Ed was like and what he thought, I'm struck that they're probably doing a much better job getting under his skin than he could have done getting under theirs. I don't think he'd disagree, though *A Fool's Progress* is studded with little poison pen sketches and sendups of some of them, all of which they seem to have taken with high good humor.

Like everyone else who has lived, Abbey can be seen as simple or complex. I tend toward the simple—his life was one long statement of a love for personal freedom and it was grounded in the literature of anarchism. He was hardly a faddish thinker. Sure, there are those seeming contradictions, but that happens with everyone. Hitler liked his dog, Pancho Villa didn't smoke or drink, John James Audubon slaughtered birds galore with his gun. I don't think Abbey was so complicated—he was just ornery. The rough edges, the sharp words, jarred a polite world of readers and politicians.

The rough edges and sharp words are pretty much all absent from the luncheon today. It is obvious that his friends and I are a lot more welcome than a live Edward Abbey would have been.

Ah, time for me to perform again. One last speaker, a nice lady it seems, and I leap up and blabber to launch her on this sea of early afternoon faces. She seems around sixty, has neatly trimmed hair, and wears a winning smile, something disappearing in my tottering nation. She begins by telling a story, and I take heart from the fact that I can still track her tale—everything must still be firing upstairs. She says there is an old man and an old woman sitting on a bench and the old man says guess how old I am. The old woman says stand up, drop your pants, now drop your shorts. She leans forward and takes a close look, thinks a moment, and snaps out the answer, "Eighty-three." The old man is amazed, and asks, "How did you know that?" She says, "You told me yesterday."

The speaker is a sex therapist and her name is Nancy Abbey—Ed's sister. She's a better writer than Ed, she allows with a smile, and I relax. Her Ed is named Eddie and he is a nice older brother who looks out for her on her first day of school. He's also lazy, always hiding up in a tree when he's supposed to be out with the rest of the family hoeing in the field. She's proud of him but not much in awe—he ain't heavy, he's just my fucking brother. A breath of fresh air. She operates beyond biography in a simpler and finer world of memory. I get letters in that vein, from people who bumped into Abbey and have etched into their memory every detail of a brief exchange in a parking lot. Harmless, I guess.

I am sitting in the southeast chair with a knife and fork and spoon and napkin in front of me. I am sipping a cup of black coffee and a bowl of steaming menudo stares up at me. He enters, walks seventeen and a half steps, and sits down. He orders two eggs, link sausage, and hash browns. He is wearing a snappy cap like those favored by motorists in old British sports cars. He looks thin and for months has not wanted his photograph taken. He will be dead in two or three weeks. He says hello and then not much else. This really happened . . . and so what?

Or I'll tell another tale. The drunks sleep under the floor of the old house where I work and at night I can hear them fluttering and mumbling as I stare into the lonely screen of a computer. I never roust the drunks lest they temporarily sober up and burn me out. I truly believe in biodiversity. I'm in that phase of the magazine called start-up which means low wages, endless hours, and an abundant salsa of crises. One time I stay all night in the office with the lights out and a loaded .45 because some supporters of an irate local politico had phoned to let me know they were going to burn my little dream to the ground. I am loving every minute of it.

Then Ed calls about having lunch and I say sure, let's meet in a greasy spoon a block away. I get there ten minutes early and, to my ire, he arrives fifteen minutes late. We drift off into the small talk of good books and bad books and hey, look at that pretty girl walking past. The environment is not on the agenda, never is, since we both know people are killing the planet and there is nothing to do but fight this trend and if we lose, well, a good fight is better than being a spectator. I know how to be neutral when I report but not when I live. Ed doesn't know how to be neutral anywhere or anytime. About the only time I can remember discussing this thing called the environment was when he mentioned that some poll showed eighty percent of the population was pro-environment. I told him the poll didn't mean shit, it was just the gesture of busy people being cornered by a pollster in some mall parking lot where they were firing up their car so they could hurry toward their second home and third wife and fifth microwave oven. He seemed a little hurt by my abrupt dismissal of this faint sign of hope.

About fifteen minutes into the meal, he mentioned the car accident by way of apologizing for his late arrival. Seems some driver had pulled out in front of him on the way down and he'd had a head-on collision. Later we went out and examined his wounded beast, an old Ford pickup with its nose a bit mangled and punched in. I said, are you hurt? and he shook his head, naw. The historical documentation of this non-event now rests on the back cover of the hardback edition of *One Life At A Time, Please*. I was there for the picture-taking, holding one of those big white disks that reflects the light just so for some kind of necessary highlights. The truck by then had a couple of plastic flowers in the hood where the vanished ornament had once been secured, and noticeably sagged on the driver's right. A perky FOR SALE sign smiled from the front windshield. Ed stood to one side looking serious about something.

The truck is sold now and I suppose in some collector's garage being tended like an oil painting by an old master. A piece of the true cross, courtesy of Detroit. There is a kind of strange animism in my culture. People seem to think that if they possess industrial products once used by another human being, they then possess something of that human being. Liberace's clothes, Judy Garland's red shoes. I am resigned to the existence of this primitive faith, but in the case of Abbey it saddens me. He did write those books and he did say what he thought in those books and he wasn't trying to found a religion or become a guru. He wanted people to think and be independent and he sure as hell wanted them to be better than he managed to be. True, he wished to be famous—the Fat Masterpiece quest—but that doesn't mean he wanted to be a celebrity, which is an industrial machine-made form of fame. If you do not wish to possess something Edward Abbey possessed, you just might understand what he was saying.

Wait a minute. What's Nancy saying now. Something about melancholia, how where she and Ed and the rest of the family lived in the hills around Home, Pennsylvania, in those hollows there was a palpable sadness that nothing could ever overcome. Not even her mother, a remarkable woman who put a deep stamp on the children's outlook and tastes. But that ground was defeated and it seemed to bequeath to the people a permanent cast of defeat. And she thinks that is why all the kids got the hell out. I believe her.

A lot of us have a hunger going on inside us. We're not trying to regain our childhood or return to the glory of our high school years. We're storming out to find a new and better world, one we've never seen, have probably fabricated, and will most likely only discover scraps of no matter how hard we search or work. Ed, I think, was that way and his whole body of work, I've got a hunch, was about how to leave Home, Pennsylvania, with a small suitcase holding a few sound values instilled in him by that dreary ground. He lit out for the territories where, with a tool kit of classical anarchism, classical music, frisky sex, bad diet, good cigars, strong drink, and winning companions, he could find or create the promised land. Turned out his idea of the promised land was shared by a surprising number of people and he got changed from Eddie Abbey to Edward Abbey.

But like all journeys it only looks clear and simple when you take the big view and is full of contradictions and noisome details when you zero in on the days and nights. The man of generous sympathies—he blurbed writers in a wanton way and seemed to try and get every manuscript published that he ever read—had a prickly side, a sensitivity to criticism and rejection that came out of those hills. He never got over not being a national writer and pretty much to the end of his days his books sold west of the Mississippi. He was rankled at being a regional author, although it's kind of nice to be a regional writer when the region is larger than most of the nations of this earth. To me, he took reviews of his books too seriously, and was from time to time irate about them. He could act like a wounded beast over a slight, and he exaggerated the attacks on himself. This is all the more striking since he wrote at a pitch and a volume that deliberately invited attack. Moderation was not his long suit. His stuff is full of jabs at people and ideas and naturally some of the folks he punched and slugged took notice.

He had an old friend named Allan Harrington. Allan went back to the very beginnings of what came to be called the beatniks. He was sprawled out in some dump in New York as Jack Kerouac wrote *On the Road* on that endless roll of fabled paper—a book which as it happened demolished one of Ed's early efforts, since he was about one hundred pages into a similar account when Kerouac's wonderful love song to America exploded in the bookstores. Allan hung out with William Bur-roughs and Allen Ginsberg when they were serious nobodies in the late forties and early fifties, and did pioneering acid con-sumption with Timothy Leary when he was still street legal at Harvard. He and Ed became friends later and he consoled Ed through a few busted marriages and bad nights. Besides, they were both novelists, Allan cranking out a string of strange yet elegant books. Allan is adamantly crazy. Once I was crossing a street with him and he tucked his arms up to his chest and scurried across like a rabbit. I said, "You act like everyone on the road is only there to try and kill you." He said, "They are."

A few months before Ed died they had a falling out. I have forgotten what over, but I think it was some criticism Allan made of something Ed wrote. Allan was heartbroken and called me up about it. And so the next time I ran into Ed, I said don't you think you can patch up this thing with Allan, he's really upset. And Ed said, no, I don't think so, I think I'll do without Allan. And there was a cold finality to it that I knew meant it was beyond any possibility of appeal. Maybe that ice I heard in his voice came out of escaping those dreary hills back in Appalachia, out of the hardness that it takes to fire up your guts enough to break the hold of a ground and a way of life that have been grinding down the locals there for genera-tions. Or, one could argue, maybe Abbey had simply made a time-motion-efficiency decision based on the fact that he knew he was a dying man and was dying a little quicker than he had scheduled. I really don't know. But I remember the coldness in his voice and it felt like the icy fist that hits when you open the door on a January morning.

And maybe that is where the red caddy came from. The ground willed it into being. I can only guess since I never asked. It seemed too natural to me to be a possible question.

When I was a kid living in an apartment in Chicago, the guy upstairs was a salesman and each year he bought a new Buick Roadmaster convertible. My father bought old junkers several times a year and when they stopped running, stripped the plates and left them beached by the curb all over Chicago. On summer nights, the guy upstairs would throw some of us neighborhood kids in the Buick—he had a son my exact age—and he'd put the top down and we'd cruise the streets of Chicago's South Side, then a savage ground inhabited by the Irish. When someone asked you where you lived, you named the parish and they instantly nodded with understanding. I remember those nights—the feel of the warm muggy air, the golden color of the street lamps, the slick sound of the tires sliding down the brick streets after an evening shower, and the rush of scents of garbage, sewers, food stands. It was the last gasp of the old-style American city before the suburbs sucked out the blood and muscle. People were everywhere, strolling down the sidewalks and sitting on the stoops, a low chorus of voices as neighbors talked, kids yelled at their games, and young punks stanced and snarled and did the early field work that resulted in all those rebels without a cause. We'd invariably wheel into a hotdog stand, and there'd suddenly be a pile of Chicago dogs buried under onions, relish, a slice of tomato, a slice of dill, the lava of mustard and ketchup, and then the big Buick would wheel out again, the radio crackling with the play-by-play of a night baseball game. All in all, the Buick offered one of the few escapes I can recall from the grim nature of a blue-collar neighborhood full of factory hands, crowded blocks, and in winter, snow blackened by coal dust. There could be an old Buick Roadmaster in my future.

All I know was Abbey loved his big, garish caddy convertible. When I told him it was worthy of a pimp, he simply glowed with pleasure. Maybe all it meant was a bit of contrariness, a jest from Mr. Zero-Population-Growth-Anti-Industrialism-Save-The-Earth-Pick-Up-A-Monkey-Wrench. I'm sure it got dull being regarded as a guru and debauched lay saint. But I suspect it came from a deeper place than the desire to make a V-8 quip. I think it came from the ground, those melancholic hills that walled one off from a greater world, came from boring chores around the house, from splitting wood, from a sense of being cut off from the larger and more vibrant flows of life. From the basic dynamo of the American personality, the love of power for power's sake, the lust for speed, the need for automobiles to supply something far beyond transportation, the night streaming past the windshield, a cold six-pack at hand, the radio roaring, a laughing woman by your side, a loaded gun close at hand under the seat, the pedal to the metal and absolutely no destination in mind. The hunger to leave something more than your footprints in the enormity of the landscape that you knife through at an amiable ninety miles an hour and not the slightest wobble from the perfect alignment. The red caddy comes naturally and that is the problem and that is what a lot of the books are about and that is why the key goes in the ignition and the red caddy fires up even though we all know it can never get us to where we have to go . . .

My God, it's over. Nancy is leaving the little lectern and moving gracefully to her seat. Time to fire up my synapses before a question-and-answer period can impale me to my chair for another eternity. Christ, with four speakers a couple of questions apiece could keep me here till well past milking time and that won't do. The audience gives off the faint rustle of restlessness that comes from too much chair time, but I'm not confident in this signal. They seem to be gluttons for punishment and if I don't intervene this could turn into a terrible masochistic rodeo.

I spring from my chair like a panther, heading off the maximum leader of the sponsoring organization. I point out that we've been here for three hours or so and that none of the panelists are too fleet of foot. In fact, anybody could pretty much tackle one and ask a question. So, I throw them upon the tender mercies of the mob and the rest of us louts, simple souls who cannot conjure up a single question, can adjourn to the bar down the hall and drink strong water.

And so it comes to pass.

More than a thousand miles off the coast, the water is just
about freezing and the waves sometimes slap through an
open window on the bridge. It's midnight or later, and there
is glow off the froth of the waves as the ship plows ahead.
Everything is cold and wet except Aquagirl, and she's busy
at the wheel right now. Blues purr from the tape machine
and for a change the engine is functioning. We've been out
here close to three weeks and I'm sick of it all. Sick of the
same twenty-three faces—except for you, Aquagirl—sick of
the miserable food, sick of everybody vomiting all the time
as tropical storms ripple through our alimentary canals and
make the ship like a teeter-totter. My only act of self-dis-
covery has been that I can't seem to get seasick. So while
vomit and other effluvia flow down the halls like a curious
tide, I've been making do with Aquagirl's staggering reserve
of white rum. For me, this has been a wondrous and unsus-
pected aspect of a woman who is a devotee of macrobiotics.

A few days ago, we finally did it. We hauled the flack
jackets and Kevlar helmets out of the sea locker, fired up the
engines, and went hunting. We were on the edge of a new
country since we also had copies of AK-47s and a nifty .50
caliber with armor-penetrating ammunition. The crew itself
was a mixed bag of animal rights people, hardball vegetari-
ans, old dopers, blue-collar workers, and whoever was on the
dock when we pulled out. Not to mention the larder of LSD
which one greedy shipmate has munched pretty much by
himself.

Mainly, like I said, it has been boring. The crew has
read itself out—a passel of Abbey's works in the galley
library. In fact, we're kind of writing another stanza in
the rollicking ballad of monkey wrenching. How did this

*evolution go? Back in the fifties, Ed and his buddies were
out knocking down billboards like a lot of other patriotic
Americans. Then somehow they moved on to decommis-
sioning bulldozers, removing surveyors' stakes, destroying
the strange apparatus of geophones and high-tech whatnot
that the Darth Vaders of mining exploration favor, spiking
trees, surgically removing slow elk, vandalizing subdivision
projects—well, one form of high jinks after another. All in
good fun, and be sure to carry a flute in your back pocket
and laugh a lot, amigo.*

*Now, as the New Age savants say, we are on the cusp
of the next stage. Killing. Good-bye, Gandhi, and I'm sure
as hell going to miss you but the eco-wars beckon and full
lotus has given way to the closed fist. It began at first light.
We'd finally located the Northern Pacific drift net fleet of
about 1500 ships, each trailing out twenty, thirty, forty
miles of net. A helluva good outfit, they manage to kill
every living thing that crosses their path and some of it is
even worth keeping and eating. It's a business in a hungry
world. The first ship we rammed seemed real surprised as
we severed the million-dollar net, smashed the hell out the
expensive gear that hauled it in, and left a nice big rent
in the hull. The second ship was less surprised—a knife
whizzed past my head. And then the bastards fled, our old
engine broke down once again, and the season was over. We
never got to fire a shot.*

*We are leaving the fishing grounds, they've kind of
made our m.o. and they stay out of our reach. That's okay,
I've had enough. I admit to feeling a grim delight when we
were wrecking things. I enjoyed striking back. But given
the scale of the problem, we were left with making gestures.*

We've got lots of videotape, which we'll feed to broadcasters
if we ever make port and then it will race around the world
for a day or two and alert everyone to what they already
know but don't like to admit: the oceans are dying. It's a
long way from having a few beers and whacking out some
billboards and it's beginning to look a lot like work.

I'm staring out the window of the bridge at the seeth-
ing nighttime sea. Aquagirl is efficient and silent as she
guides the old tub through the vast ocean and her blonde
hair glows in the strange light, a small and nice case of St.
Elmo's fire. She's a spirited person, had to get her out of the
clink just before we shipped. She tells me she came out here
to die and now she's fucked up that simple ambition since she
seems pretty damned alive. She doesn't know much about
this Abbey fellow but when I tell her a few things she allows
he doesn't sound half bad. But of course he's not why anyone
is here. To start with, he's dead. Besides that, this was all in
the cards anyway. It's a hydra-headed monster popping up
all over the place. Abbey kind of gave it a form and tried to
fashion an ethic for it. But he didn't start it—or claim to—
and I don't know who or what is going to end it. But I know
it's headed toward killing. Well, the hell with those thoughts
for now. It's a beautiful evening, the waves whoosh with a
nice slapping sound against the old hull, the ship is largely
asleep and the entire universe is this bridge, Aquagirl, and
the sea around us.

Suddenly, a whale dives before us—did we disturb its
sleep? The beast glows in the soft wet night as it vanishes
under the waves. Sober, I hear the faint sound of a radio
playing classical music. I stand up, gain my sea legs, and
look down near the prow. A red caddy whips by, coursing

over the tops of the waves, and the reckless driver never even looks back. We could have had a serious collision. I'm stunned. I knew that model had electric windows but not a hydro-power system.

I order the first drink of many. I have traversed some kind of minefield and I am still not certain just what I have been dodging and fearing. Friends drift in, people from Abbey's books and people from Abbey's trenches. It will be all right, it will all mellow out. I can sense my bar bill is going to march toward a hundred bucks or more—must be a good host or I'll disappoint my father.

Things begin to get blurry, thank God. And then I notice a suicide blonde has magically appeared and is draining double vodkas at the speed of light. She seems to have had a good head start, to boot. She's a trim woman of about thirty years and as near as I can track her story, she's been pitched out of a half dozen schools, but not to worry, Dad keeps finding her a new and innocent institution and bankrolling her education. Turns out she's a serious fan of the late author. Her speech is studded with profanity in a winsome way. Beneath her bravado lingers the small delights and smiles of a little girl and I am heartened that nothing to date has extinguished this freshness and it is still swimming boldly through her riptide of vodka.

Oh, she wants to know about him and talk about his books and make herself feel good. I lean back in my chair and let others take over the task at hand. I can find nothing wrong with her—at least nothing that she wouldn't admit to herself. She wants to believe, she wants to find a way to make a dent in a wayward world, and right now she also wants to get smashed. She's come to the right place.

I catch a vaguely familiar face out of the corner of my eye but I cannot seem to place it. A middle-aged balding man gets up from a table and lumbers over to me. He says his name and I realize I've known him since we were both twelve years old, although there has been a brief break in our relationship of about twenty years. I rise and join him and what turns out to be his now-grown daughter, his new wife, and a baby he's adopted from his recent spiritual trek in the Himalayas. The parents sold him the child both for money, which is understandable, and because they were starving to death and wanted to launch one of their number into the cosmos of hope.

My friend is in flight from death. He's recently had the "big one"—his family tree is cursed with fatal heart disease—and his circling of the globe has now almost been completed and the new babe in arms marks both his defiance and his acceptance of death. He'll go, but in a manner that suggests his own idea of fighting. He has been seriously mired in Oriental religions for decades so adoption fits him better than combat. I feel a fine glow. I have never seen a live baby who made me think of overpopulation—the dead ones with flies on their faces in all those Mexican villages, those I refuse to deal with at the moment. Just like I refuse to deal with a smart son of a friend of mine who lives against the Sierra Madre and lives from pillar to post. When this son went to work at ten, I protested, but when he finally left the classroom for back-breaking labor at twelve there was nothing I could do—even though the kid was smart as a whip.

My friend starts talking to me of his coronary and his rebirth—we pretty much skip the twenty-year gap and neither of us shows much interest in catching up on the trivia of our lives. He is one of those blessed people made more alive by a near-death experience. He oozes tender feelings and I can sense that the baby is life to him. It's a long trip from our boozy days in whorehouses and our spacey nights riding magic carpets of dope. The baby sucks—the adoptive mother has somehow jump-started her breasts—and we laugh and talk and ignore death. Death is inevitable but what my friend and his wife have done is not inevitable. I look down at the brown face with black hair and hear a gurgling sound that is hope itself . . .

I had little to do with the dying and most of that little I did not understand at the time. Anyway, it's all drifted into legend now. I think he half-orchestrated it that way—that manic need for control that seems to possess novelists with their made-up worlds, where people say what they tell them to say. Or maybe it was a fool's luck, to cap a fool's progress. Let's go over the schedule. He calls early in the week and says let's go camping Thursday. Then I call Wednesday night and say I can't make it, too much work, I don't feel good. He gently insists I go anyway—he's got a friend down from New Mexico he wants me to meet. Nope, can't do it, Ed. Thursday unbeknownst to me he goes under the knife. Friday, I drop by his house and discover from Clarke he's lying in a hospital bed all cut up. Then it gets blurry for me.

Clarke calls early in the morning and says Ed just died. I ask if she needs help and she says no, it's all being taken care of. I don't inquire about the details because I've got a pretty good idea. I can see in my mind's eye the truck bed, the body wrapped in something, the shovels, the load of ice. The phone starts ringing and for the next few hours I become obituary central, babbling to microphones, firing off copy to various rags. Then I shut it down, walk two blocks, and buy a gallon of red wine. I go out into the yard under the hackberry tree, sit, and drink. The phone keeps ringing but I do not answer it. When the message tape periodically fills, I hit erase and let it start feeding all over again.

None of this is a surprise. I'm just not ready for it. I've done my civic chores—faxed all the publications their red meat and told them to send the check to Earth First! (I still remember with pleasure the pleading voices on the line asking if they *had* to send the money there.)

Abbey had been dying in his cheerful way for years. I love the story of when he came to from his pancreatic crisis a decade earlier and the doc told him he had maybe six months. He supposedly said, "Well, I guess I don't have to floss anymore." Makes a great story. And then this last project of his, the sequel to *The Monkey Wrench Gang*, had an admittedly rushed quality about it. Ed had told me he was, alas, going to have to finally really work and I lined up a hideaway for him so he could crank out the pages fast. I'd get notes from him complaining about the unseemly pace and lamenting that he was turning into a dull brute like me. Then one night he called for technical details about the operation of an Uzi, explaining it played a part in the big trial section that wrapped up the novel. Then he finished the book and there was no trial section at all. Sometimes things make one change plans a bit.

He wakes up in the hospital after the operation and the surgeons have not pulled the hat trick. So he unplugs himself from the medicine machine, clambers out of bed, and goes off with Clarke and friends into the desert to die. Naturally, he failed— he was not good at deadlines—and finally the next morning gets the job done on the floor of his writing shack. Then comes the call.

I keep drinking steadily, bestirring myself periodically to erase the phone messages from the twitching ganglia of the national media. Later that day someone penetrates my solitude under the hackberry and drags me off to a saloon where she kindly pours more booze down my throat and speaks in a soft and gentle way. I am not fit company and I know it. I direct her to a supermarket where I purchase another gallon of fuel and a car trails us to my hut. I stumble up the path to the door, carefully avoiding the cactus and the softly swaying branches of the paloverde. I hear footsteps. It is a reporter, the very same one whom years before I'd field marshaled against Ed during his crafty attempt to rezone his land. She says I'll understand because this is just business. She needs to know the *real* cause of death. Real? What is this shit? His heart stopped beating and then he got cold and became clinically dead. Isn't that enough?

No, no, she says, the public has a right to know. Public? Who the fuck is this public? I've never met the public in all the thousands of people I've bumped up against. Slowly, it dawns on me what this public has a right to know. Ummm, was it AIDS? Perhaps a tasty suicide?

I have had a lot to drink and will have a lot more before my night is finished but I think that has nothing to do with what happens next. I will not blame the bottle. I start pushing her off my tiny patch of the earth and then somehow I have this vague memory of her going kind of airborne over a hedge. And then I am in the street and she is bolting into her car and hitting the door locks with panic in her eyes. I was told later there was talk of a lawsuit by the newspaper. Could be. I'm not proud of my behavior. I hate violence, especially my own.

The thing, though, will not die. Years later a friend tells me that a reporter interviewed him and asked why he didn't tell the real truth about Abbey, that he had committed suicide. My friend was stunned, and said because that is not true. But the reporter knew better and scoffed at this tame answer.

I think I know why there is this need for a certain death. He can't be allowed to have gotten away with it. He must get his comeuppance for all that hard talk of his.

Well, I'm sorry. I don't think Ed was happy to die but I think he died happy, or as happy as Ed could be. After all, he always had a lot on his mind . . .

I'm cruising the Colorado plateau in a truck at about ninety.
It is late afternoon and Gallup is coming up alarmingly fast.
The red caddy is often moored there—whatever that may
mean, since it often seems to slip its anchor. I've grown used
to its belligerent and ill-mannered appearance. It passed
me a while ago just as I came up on a wire-caged walkway
over the interstate. A drunken Indian was standing atop the
cage and tottering over four lanes of intercontinental traffic
while a young woman reached up to him with a pleading
look in her eyes and brushed her fingers against the stiff wire
on which he stood. Outside of Gallup, I follow a stream of
exiting cars to some kind of amphitheater lodged in a red
rock wall. The parking lot is full and as I walk toward the
main event I see the caddy left all akimbo on a sidewalk. I
waltz through the gate and notice a herd or two of menacing
cops complete with dope dogs and loaded batons.

Down in the pit some heavy metal band is thrashing
out harmonics and a small mob of kids is slam dancing in
the afternoon sun. Young women walk past with blank eyes,
tattoos, large breasts and a perfume that kills hope with
one whiff. The young men shuffle past with homicide eyes.
I am staring into the triumph of the industrial revolution,
complete with cleavage. Here are all the people no factory
whistle calls.

I lean against a railing and then walk on, eyeing a
couple of tough mommas with death-rock makeup, pins
through their noses, and bodies that stretch their clothes
beyond the normal tensile limits of fabrics. Suddenly some
asshole walks into me and as I reel and regain my balance
I see some graybearded old fart with a dipshit sports hat
disappearing into the mob. I'm outta here.

Roar north past Shiprock, hang a left into the Diné
heart and put the pedal down. Hello cock's comb, cluck

under the chin for baby rocks, skip the lethal Navajo tacos
of Kayenta. I'm impressed by what sheep can do to good ole
Mom Earth—nobody has to worry about mowing the weeds
here. Crack another bottle and turn off on a dirt track,
carefully skirting the hogans. Park, stagger out, piss, now
up the sandy hill. The old building stands roofless with
soldier graffiti cut in the walls from the mid-nineteenth
century. Everybody seemed to miss their girl. I sit down and
gaze at the abandoned village site below. The highway is a
two-lane ribbon in the middle distance said to be lined with
Navajo ghosts, the spirits of dead drunks who were heading
toward one more off-reservation bottle. They say at night
they'll beckon you and you'll go flying off the road to your
death.

I see a red streak slash down the highway and then
hear the distant sound of an obscene cackle. Well, fuck you,
asshole.

I stumble down the hill slippin'-and-a-slidin' and hit
the cut of a hungry arroyo. I bumble down it until I come to
a cut bank with bones sticking out. Old ones sleep here. Sure
enough, two grave sites are being excavated by the rains,
Anasazi skeletons that have been snoring the best part of this
millennium. Should be a nice valuable pot under the skull
of each one of these stiffs. Collectors pay a small fortune
for these babies. When the next rain comes the waters will
lift them from their resting place and the old pots will bob
on the waves and then smash against things and break into
fragments. In time they'll be nothing at all but little fragments and then the fragments will be ground down into dust.
Sounds fine to me.

I leave them. I'm not cut out to be a grave robber.
Besides, the idea of the grave and the tenderness of pots as
an offering are what count with me.

Night does not help. I'm still drinking. That does not help either. Outside, the trees stir faintly, the desert breathes, sighs, gurgles and now and then belches. It has no manners. I know where the burial site is and I used to go there a lot. So did he. Kind of a home base before the leap into the great beyond. I've never returned since he was planted. Maybe I hate littering. I'd tell you more about it except for the long-distance calls late at night from people I don't know. The voices are real friendly and they sound like likable folks. They've read his stuff it turns out and they have questions. Like where is he buried?

I never tell them. Not that it matters, I figure it'll get out, probably already has from what I can gather. It is a human question and I do not mean to mock. But still it repels me. What does the grave matter except to the occupant? And I'm not real sure he's around there much anyway. He's off being that bullshit vulture he always wanted to be. Or maybe that prankster that he always was, diving on my bird feeder as a peregrine. I don't have time for this mumbo-jumbo. Got a world to save, miles to go, hello Miss, and what is your name? Besides I want to learn Thai cooking, start a private nature park, and win the lottery. No time. What do you mean, ass-hole, by "that silly magazine"?

Missed the big requiem in Arches too. Not good at sched-ules. Once in a while I have a beer with people who knew him—not often—and after a few cold ones we shyly admit to this preposterous feeling that he is not dead, that we've caught sight of him in some crowd, a brief glimpse from the corner of our eyes. And then we always laugh and ridicule ourselves. Damn foolishness. Look, I know he's deader than a doornail because I liked him, and I've never been fond of leaders or gurus, much less gods. So he is dead. Or I am a damn poor judge of character. Still, there is this strange sense that he is not done, that he is still out and about. Maybe that is what the boom in the sale of his books is about. Like Elvis, Ed made a great career move.

Ah, he's safe now. In fact, he is government approved. I'll tell you a true story. There is a cabinet member who agrees to do a thirty-minute interview with a reporter friend of mine. The member's office is very grand—it is famous for its size and splendor even in the world of cabinet members. My friend is struck that the man's press secretary is not in attendance. This has never happened before and indicates possibly a very serious discussion or an honor of unprecedented scale. The officer has indicated no calls are to be put through while he is talking, except of course that one from Nelson Mandela. But when it finally comes, even that one is relatively brief. And the half hour spills out into an hour, and the hour into two hours, and then they are in their third hour. The talk is very good, my friend's tape machine is whirring. He is getting his story, that inside stuff we all crave. And then finally, the phone rings— what? Hasn't this been forbidden?—and it is the member's secretary reminding him of his appointment with his barber. Ah, they must all go, my friend the reporter, the cabinet member, the bodyguards, the driver, must go right now. A haircut.

But the talk continues and now the man is sitting in a barber's chair and his mind is floating free, his thoughts are leaping like gazelles. Suddenly, he starts talking about Abbey's death and how Ed's friends took the body out into the desert and threw it into a hole, just like that. No big deal. That's the point the cabinet member wants to make. Do you know, he asks, that formaldehyde is incredibly toxic? And one chemical company has a lock on its manufacture. So what then are cemeteries? Toxic waste dumps, land consumers, places of poison. And these environmentalists, these radical-holier-than-thou types, do they ever mention this? No! Never! We all need to be cremated, the cabinet officer concludes. Or at least buried like Abbey, quickly and without a massive infusion of poisonous embalming fluid.

Abbey dead now lives in the very seat of government. He is leading a crusade against embalmers, he is an advocate of cremation. He is safe. That's the nice thing about being dead. People can finally talk about you. And he is famous. I'll tell you just how famous: the reporter interviewing the cabinet member is the very same reporter with whom I once had the preposterous conversation in which I went on forever about Edward Abbey and he thought I meant Abbie Hoffman. But now he has heard of Edward Abbey and he can follow the busy mind of a cabinet officer when the man uses him as a basic reference point in sorting out the toxic waste dump implications of our burying grounds. Fame, I tell you.

It is late at night and the program is over and in case you want to know, it's been an unprecedented success. They blew the doors off and made a ton of money for the cause. They're talking about making it an annual event—I say no thanks.

I just keep drinking to almost no worthwhile result. I'm not sure what is happening. I've buried a healthy number of people. Eight months ago a woman I'd known for years died of cancer at forty-two. She left a passel of young kids, a lot of unfinished dreams. Hit me like a fist in the guts and I didn't spill a tear.

A funny thing happens on the way to the morning. I am sitting there in the dark by myself under that same hackberry tree downing one after the other when I start talking out loud. I say I feel corrupted, I say I feel I violated a dead friend, I say I feel I cut him up and sold him like cuts of meat in a butcher shop. I say I feel dirty. And I break down and sob endlessly—at least it seems pretty damn endless to me. I'm not good at crying. Like many males, I lack practice, lack the ability to acknowledge what I feel.

(Even as I write this I feel myself distancing myself from the way my tears flowed ceaselessly as I babbled things I understood but could neither explain nor track down to their true source. What had I done, for Christ's sake? Hosted a literary luncheon to remember, and remember fondly, a dead friend.)

So what is all this crying?

It's partly that I feel alone. But mainly it is that I don't want to remember him because I cannot forget him. And he wasn't a saint. And he wasn't a mentor. And he wasn't a hero. And he wasn't my only friend. And if he was one of a kind we are all in worse shape than I imagined.

He lived in a moral universe. Beneath all the sexist barbs, the racist wit, the meanness, the pranks, the stunts, the anger, the episodes, the constant laughter and mirth, he inhabited and consciously expanded a moral universe. One where cleverness and normal standards of success don't count for much but right and wrong count for pretty much everything. Ah, one life at a time, please, but still a real life. When he was around there were things I blew off because I knew Abbey, diligent sap that he was, would take up my slack. Now I can't say that to myself.

And I have a hard time maintaining his sense of the absurd. Back in the fun days when he was pretending to be Morton Kamins, his brilliant profiler, he objected to the way critics treated him and his work:

> "It's really a form of play, this writing of books," Abbey continues. "And if the reviewers, especially those literal-minded androgynes in New York, ever took a close look

at my books, they'd find that they consist mostly of play.
Play! for Christ's sake!"

Okay, Ed, playtime. I'll try more regularly to be an asshole.

So no gravesite visits. No more programs. No more requiems, memorials, monuments. No nothing. Everything that matters I can carry within me. Nobody needs to go looking for Edward Abbey, he's everywhere now. He's just sporting a different name. He didn't leave disciples or followers, at least I hope not. Nor did he clone himself. At best he sketched a way of looking at things that a lot of people in the West already felt—he just made what we felt and thought and sensed into words. And he gave us a few laughs along the way. So we don't need another one of him, there's tens of thousands of maniacs like him out there right this moment. And I'm afraid somebody better alert the authorities—I'm finding more Abbeys everyday.

I'm sitting in the backyard now, squaring off with a stone statue of Saint Francis. A green serpentine Jamaican cactus crawls across his chest and two stone birds rest on his shoulders, one more perches on his folded hands. He's got a face like Frankenstein and I suspect this is deliberate. The peasant who carved him for me had a terrific sense of mockery. Dribs and drabs of bird shit caress his stone hide and his eyes are, well, monstrous. On favored nights, and this is not one of them, the cactus explodes with dozens of big white blooms and by morning the yard sags under the crushing weight of tropical scent. It is like walking into pure sex. Not safe sex, not the skin magazines, not talk about relationships, not manners, not morals, but that deeper thing, the flow—is it a river? a jet stream? a big syringe full of hormones?—that courses through our lives, that very thing we hide with language, clothing, customs and laws. But that we cannot always hide with our eyes. Flowers don't seem to hide it at all. And of course flowers are not into fidelity, the cactus-stroking Saint Francis beckons any big moth or bat that catches a whiff of the fragrance. And of course flowers are not into planned parenthood, but cast down hundreds or thousands of seeds in the hope of . . . of something no flower will say and no human knows how to ask. This musk, mess, mayhem. We can't admit, we can't deny it. The disorder, but . . . please, touch me, hold me and if you must speak, whisper. We'll call it love and then we will feel better. But we will call it, again and again, against our will we will say. But we will call. This thing of darkness or of light—it really depends on what kind of eyes you have or what kind of lens you wear to doctor those eyes. They tell me it can launch a thousand ships, throw up a Taj Mahal, and scare the horses, too.

So I'm sitting here. This is where the video crew interviewed me for the tape I have never removed from the plastic wrap, much less watched. I'm not sure what I said and naturally have no idea what the director picked from the things I said.

It was a delicious moment. I was deep into writing a book on Charlie Keating, a banker who failed to the tune of two billion dollars or so and is now spending his golden years in the joint. A man Ed despised and I liked and was fascinated by. There is a knock at the door, I rise half-crazed from my computer, and they trudge in with tripod and gear. They scout the house, ah, they decide on the yard. It is a jumble of trees and flowers and shrubs, a landscape but not a garden. They plop down a chair and say, here, sit right here. The day is sunny and my head is full of financial records, felonies, acts of betrayal, the normal effluvia of corporate life.

The producer asks a question and I answer. I can hear this rumble coming out of me, a creature is talking who sometimes visits my life and sounds like a laconic Old Testament prophet who could do with a little dope and a pretty girl. Lighten up, fellow. But it is no use, I seem to thunder on. Soon I suspect there will be heat lightning, then possibly the vicious hail that makes a mash of the knee-high corn and destroys all hope of a crop or of meeting the big bank loan on the home place.

My mouth says God knows what and my heart goes back to a night when Abbey slouched in to address an Earth First! rally. He was wearing that damn sports cap for his new life as a caddy owner and had the sheaf of paper he needed as a crutch if he was going to give a speech—hell, he didn't really give speeches, he just read at people. There was a whole raft of performers that night, a folk singer named Katie Lee who was a friend of mine, a poet who chanted out some poems, and others. I was about to launch the first issue of my "silly little magazine," as Ed put it, and I had dragged my business partner along so that he could get educated on all of the complications and little byways of the life of our town. The crowd was woodsy, flannel shirts, jeans, clunky boots, no makeup on the women, hair on the faces of the men. Basically up against the wall, muthafucka, we've come for your dozer.

Finally, Ed's turn came and he stumbled up to the front of the room and began to read an excerpt from something he had been scribbling. My memory is not crystal clear but his tale seemed to come from his student days in New Mexico and involved quite a bit of wild pistol shooting from speeding cars, some strong drink and the loving ministrations of squads of uniformly blonde sorority girls who were uninhibited and, at least in his recollection, possessed a quite tender touch. The audience grew quite still and their silence did not seem to me to flow from reverence. But I could be wrong—perhaps they did consider blonde, loving sorority girls an essential element of biodiversity, kind of like cobras and bubonic plague. Finally, Ed stopped his droning and there was polite applause and he strode back to where I was leaning against a wall in the rear.

I said something like, "Congratulations."

And he said something like, "Why, what do you mean?" And he was wearing this shit-eating grin. Ah, my boy.

Whoops, the director is asking me another question, I shift gears and then after, what?—ten minutes? an hour?—they shut off the camera. It's a wrap. All done and tidy. I apologize, as is my custom whenever these historic film and tape events occur, and we stand around just talking. Turns out the guy running the camera once flew in Charlie Keating's lavish helicopter and I leap into working speed and start making notes as I pump him dry. And then they go out the door to do yet more interviews. And now I'm sitting in the same yard and it's a different year and it is night and I've never watched the videotape and I'm calming down.

You know, I increasingly think there is something to this peregrine business. To begin with, he'd be likely to put down this false trail of vulture bullshit. Probably got Morton Kamins on the case right now, spewing out pages of disinformation. I tell you, he was not always trustworthy. But peregrines dive at up to 200 mph, and they've got incredible eyes that can zoom in and out. People coddle them also, they're damn near a cult since the DDT scare and many a helping hand is providing perches and sanctuary. They go everywhere, too, from the wildest, baddest wilderness to the heart of the most wretched city. Christ, they're diving right in my own yard. No manners, none at all. Right now, everyone kind of likes peregrines— except of course those creatures they kill and then rip to shreds.

They are literally free. If you ever have the good fortune to see one, especially one diving toward a kill, they will from that moment onward become your felt definition of the word freedom. Think on it.

So, it could be he's pissing away his time up there in the sky. Frankly, I'll bet on a peregrine over a vulture. Vultures, while friendly creatures, are much too passive. They wait for someone else to do the work and put dinner on the table. I once spent a week or so with vultures while they totally disassembled a dead coyote. They were great neighbors but you are never likely to kiss them—strictly talk-over-the-fence kind of neighbors. They're clubby by nature and pretty much do everything as a group. I'll be very surprised if vultures ever produce a major writer. They're simply too well balanced for such an activity. Sure, they could be critics, but it's not likely they'll turn into real writers.

. . . Blurring, the blurring, it is everywhere in the literature. You are cruising so high in the sky as to be invisible, barely a dot, and yet you can see. Your eye is unique, it is better than the very best lens on a camera, it can effortlessly zoom in and out and yet the focus never fails, the distortion is minimal, almost nonexistent. A rabbit moves, or perhaps a mouse, maybe a small bird, and you stoop, fold in your wings, and plummet toward the earth. Speed picks up, 100 mph, now 130 mph, and you are suddenly hitting 180 mph, the earth is screaming up at you, but the eye holds, locks in on the target in a manner all the world's warlords envy. No cyborg yet imagined can equal your vision, not a one, and the view is clear, hard-edged, the blurring is something you never experience. You see truly, the rabbit moves, you pull out of your dive four inches off the surface of the earth, the talons lock on your prey, the impact kills instantly, you fly off to your perch where your woman waits. And that is breakfast, the start of a new day. There is no blurring, you see truly, although no one believes your reports. They pretend they do not exist. Blurring, the blurring, it is everywhere in their literature . . .

Peregrines are birds of a different feather. They lack patience. Outside of courtship, they seem to live solitary lives. We seldom see them, they live beyond our vision and comprehension. So high in the sky, and there is the matter of velocity. They've essentially come back from the dead against all expectations. And anyone who has ever seen a peregrine in action knows they drive too damn fast.

*Patience is wearing thin. Night has dropped like a ton of
bricks but still the truck roars on. The new bottle was hard
to crack what with the driving, but it's open now. Out there
hums a marvel of modern times, the Black Mesa electric
trolley. A train that carries coal from Black Mesa to Page,
Arizona, the town cheek-to-jowl with Glen Canyon Dam.
Behind the dam, under the waters of Lake Powell, sleep
110 dead canyons. The train hauls endless cars of coal to the
power plant at Page that helps generate the juice to make
everything run in these, and more distant, parts. Thirty
years have passed since the last nail was driven into the
coffin and the train works day and night moving those tens of
thousands of tons of fuel to keep the beast fed.*

    *Have a swig, can't run the world you know. Abbey
used to drive down this road blowing the insulators off the
power poles. Stupid thing to do. Hardly made a dent in the
bastards. Big wires keep on humming. The window is open
and the desert breeze feels warm, and rich with night scent.
It is good to be alive. But then, it always is.*

    *The flash from the barrel is alarming, the brilliant
yellow flame and then the smell of gunpowder. Hope no one
notices, but every job has its hazards. The bullets hit with a
dull thud on the cars carrying the coal. Any fool could hit
them. In the morning they'll be walking around the yards
and notice these weird dimples in the metal sides and think
what the hell caused this? More planning is required. Obvi-
ously, metal jacketed rounds from a larger caliber would
penetrate the metal walls of the cars and it stands to reason
might ignite the coal. Imagine an entire slave train rolling
through the night afire, the flames eating out the entrails of
the beast. Worth a shot.*

    What the hell, a maniac coming up behind? A

drunken Indian? The authorities? A blur of red streams past, the top is down on some behemoth of a convertible, and there is this old geezer sitting at the wheel firing one pistol after another—he tosses them aside like Kleenex when he empties a magazine—at the train. The caliber sounds inadequate, isn't going to do anything but cause harmless dents in the side. Besides, with the top down he's in plain view. What kind of a goddamn fool is this?

Better get his shit together before he gets killed. This ain't a game, mister.

AAA Route Guide

Never before in history have slaves been so well fed, thoroughly medicated, lavishly entertained—but we are all slaves nonetheless. Our debased popular culture—television, rock music, home video, processed food, mechanical recreation, wallboard architecture—is the culture of slaves. Furthermore, the whole grandiose structure is self-destructive: by enshrining the profit motive (power) as our guiding ideal, we encourage the intensive and accelerating consumption of land, air, water—the natural world—on which the structure depends for its continued existence. A house built on greed will not long endure. Whether it's called capitalism or socialism makes little difference. Both of these oligarchic, militaristic, expansionistic, acquisitive, industrializing, and technocratic systems are driven by the same motives; both are self-destroying. Even without the accident of nuclear war, I predict that the military-industrial state will disappear from the surface of the earth within a century. That belief is the basis of my inherent optimism, the source of my hope for the coming restoration of a higher civilization: scattered human populations modest in number that live by fishing, hunting, food-gathering, small-scale farming, and ranching, that gather once a year in the ruins of abandoned cities for great festivals of moral, spiritual, artistic, and intellectual renewal, a people for whom wilderness is not a playground but their native home.

New dynasties will arise, new tyrants will appear—no doubt. But we must and we can resist such recurrent aberrations by keeping true to the earth and remaining loyal to our basic animal nature. Humans were free before the word *freedom* became necessary. Slavery is a cultural invention. Liberty is life: *eros* plus *anarchos* equals *bios*.

"Long live democracy. Two cheers for anarchy."

Acknowledgments

I want to thank all the people who helped me write this and all the people who will help write the rest of it.

Over the years I've known quite a few people who, not unnaturally, also knew Edward Abbey—many of them for far more years than I did, and far better, I suspect. And I've spent a lot of time over coffee or beers listening to them talk about him, a richly varied talk. Basically, most Abbey stories tend to emerge as tales about some semi-impossible beast they knew.

For years, I lived with big dogs, Newfoundlands and a Great Pyrenees, and the animals, while quite intelligent and friendly, took over my life. To begin with, they constantly judged me and, alas, I could sense from time to time found me wanting. They also tended to be quiet but when aroused made sounds like thunder. But mainly, what I recall is that the dogs—Job, Scannon, and Ben—while reasonable, had no truck with being ordered around. I could negotiate with them and ask politely but if they determined I was wrong, or morally in error, they would refuse to act on my request. When people talk to me about Edward Abbey, their tales generally remind me of the stories I used to tell about these dogs who condescended to live with me—all too briefly, for my taste. We need dogs that live longer and politicians who live a dog's life.

While Abbey was not a dog—a goal for a next life, perhaps—he was polite and soft-spoken as a rule, but fundamentally willful. You could neither control him nor tell him what to do. Not a bad trait if kept generally within the bounds of the felony statutes. And this characteristic sings out when people talk about him—a kind of cheerful resignation to a sometimes volatile reality. I've tried not to expropriate these memories, partly because they did not happen to me, and mainly because they are the memories and comforts that in all honesty belong to others.

But all the beers and cups of coffee and tales leave their mark, and I want to thank the people who have talked with me over the years. Their experiences and feelings have without doubt colored and informed this memoir. I'm sure Ed would be astounded by the number of people who recall some chance encounter with him. And I think it would please him. We all want to leave some mark in this world beyond the cruel scars that seem a good part of our species' fate.

Sources for Quotes

pages 19, 25–26, 37, 44, and 98
Edward Abbey, *One Life at a Time, Please* (New York: Henry Holt & Co., 1988).

pages 46–47
Edward Abbey, *Beyond the Wall* (New York: Holt, Rinehart, and Winston, 1984).

page 54
Review by Ed Marston in the *National Review* and quoted in Jim Bishop, Jr., *Epitaph for a Desert Anarchist: The Life and Legend of Edward Abbey* (New York: Atheneum, 1994).

pages 54 and 88–89
From Morton Kamins, "Son of the Desert," a three-thousand-word manuscript in the Abbey Collection, Special Collections, University of Arizona.